Praise for the Positive Discipline Series

"I was guilty of pampering my son, making excuses for him, and underestimating his abilities. Furthermore, I had not put him 'in the boat' with my other child. I had somehow arrived at believing that he did in fact have 'special' needs—when, really, he has the very same needs as all children: to belong and to feel significant. Reading this book helped me to realize that I rarely (if ever) asked my son how he was *feeling*. Now I do that as common practice. The culture of autism is a real thing, and our family battles against its grip daily. If autism threatens to impair his ability to communicate and interact, we push back. But my son should not be a casualty in that game of tug-of-war. This book asks us to project thirty years into the future and imagine the child as an adult. In completing the exercise, I examined my own wishes: *What do I want?* Your book provided my response: I want him to belong and to feel significant. I can't 'control' autism, and I can't make promises for a future that is not my own. However, I can work on those wishes now and ensure that my son feels important and loved and heard every day. And this will no longer be done by pampering him or making excuses, but by encouraging him to ask for help, to stretch his boundaries, to have even higher expectations for what I know he can accomplish, and to love him unconditionally—not because he is my child with special needs but because he is my child."
—**Amy Azano, Ph.D., Curry School of Education, University of Virginia**

"A wonderful resource for parents and teachers . . . provides an important guide toward understanding children's behavior and the underlying communication it represents. It explains a very exciting set of tools for eliciting the best from children with difficult behaviors by transforming those behaviors into clearer and more direct communication. . . . Parents and teachers of children with special needs should look no further for the help they have wanted to bring more harmony and comfort into their challenging lives."
—**Deborah Herzberg, school psychologist**

"Positive Discipline teaches us a new way to view the child's behavior. The book informs us, professionals and parents, that some of the behaviors and 'mistakes' of special needs children are innocent. We learn that the very behavior that is causing power struggles and distress to the family is part of the child's disability. With this knowledge and with the tools of Positive Discipline, we can approach our children with greater understanding and, consequently, have fewer power struggles."
—**Hilde Price-Levine, LCSW**

"I am thrilled that someone finally got it right!!! There are numerous books in the stores that speak about how to identify a child with special needs, but few that give examples and the tools to help parents and teachers handling challenging situations. I just about did a cartwheel when you said in your introduction that many just want to manage these children as opposed to understand them. Loved it!!!"

—Kim Dillon, parent educator, Raleigh, North Carolina

"This book is exceptional. . . . The authors show deep sensitivity to the inner world of children with special needs and present fine-tuned interventions which honor the individual child. They respectfully show the growth in the adults learning to use positive discipline techniques. The concepts presented in this book are professional and educational; however, the format and the language used to explain them is easily understood by a wide range of parents and teachers."

—Nancy Lamb, Ph.D., psychologist

"Positive Discipline's relational and child-centered approach is intuitive, proven, empathic, and 'brain-based'—focusing on promoting social-emotional competencies and solving social-behavioral challenges for *all* children with any special need."

—David W. Willis, MD, FAAP, behavioral-developmental pediatrics, Medical Director, Artz Center for Developmental Health and Audiology, Portland, Oregon

"After forty years of experience working with children with special needs, it is refreshing to find a book that recognizes that every child needs to be treated as an individual with a potential for success—especially a child with special needs. This book leads the way with an exciting strength-based approach—including a clear framework and practical tools. It's sure to be a source of information and encouragement for parents."

—Mary Jamin Maguire, MA, LP, LICSW

"As an education professor, I reinforce with my future teachers the idea that all students' answers to questions, right or wrong, have an internal logic. We as teachers must discover that logic before we help a child to discover other ways of approaching the question. What I love about this volume is the recognition of the logic within *all* children and the commitment to listening to the child with all our senses as we help them to move beyond misdirected behaviors. . . . On a personal level, reading this manual reminded me of how to access my higher self in all my relationships. . . . I recommend this book most highly."

—Peter R. Thacker, Ph.D., Associate Professor, School of Education, University of Portland

"[This book] is based on the premise that all human beings have a need to belong and be connected to others. Kids with special needs are no different, yet we so often have the mistaken view that they are, which can result in a distorted view of a child's potential. We all feel better about ourselves when we feel competent and appreciated, and kids are the same way. . . . This book reminds us to keep a long-term vision in mind: *All* children deserve to know they are loved and important, and that they have the ability to bring joy and meaning to the lives of others."

—Linda Dorzweiler, Associate Director,
Clackamas County Children's Commission Head Start

"Written in a style that is practical, relevant, and effective, this book offers insights and guidance for parents and is a must-read for professionals that work with children that have special needs."

—Nocona Pewewardy, MSW, Ph.D., Assistant Professor,
Portland State University School of Social Work

"The information and stories make for easy reading. The writers invite the reader to implement the information into their own lives."

—Debbie Stedman, Head Start teacher

"Offers parents a range of strategies to help strengthen their relationships with their children while interacting more positively when challenging behaviors occur. . . . The stories in [this book] are powerful everyday experiences that are transformative when we look at the situation from the child's perspective and when we apply the right tools to address our children's needs."

—David Allen, Ph.D., Portland State University

ALSO IN THE POSITIVE DISCIPLINE SERIES

POSITIVE DISCIPLINE

FOR CHILDREN WITH SPECIAL NEEDS

Raising and Teaching
All Children to Become Resilient,
Responsible, and Respectful

JANE NELSEN, ED.D., STEVEN FOSTER, LCSW, AND ARLENE RAPHAEL, MS

THREE RIVERS PRESS · NEW YORK

KH

Published in the United States by Three Rivers Press, an imprint of the
Crown Publishing Group, a division of Random House, Inc., New York.
www.crownpublishing.com

Three Rivers Press and the Tugboat design are registered
trademarks of Random House, Inc.

Cataloging-in-Publication Data is on file with the Library of Congress.

ISBN 978-0-307-58982-8
eISBN 978-0-307-58983-5

Printed in the United States of America

Book design by Cynthia Dunne
Interior illustrations by Diane Durand
Cover design by Misa Erder
Cover photography by PhotoAlto/Sigrid Olsson

10 9 8 7 6 5 4 3 2 1

First Edition

9/2/11

Jane's Dedication
Unconditional love and support—his name is Barry.

Steven's Dedication
This book is dedicated with much love and endless gratitude to my wife, Jean, and my daughter, Jordan.

Arlene's Dedication
I dedicate my writing contributions to my beloved parents, Mary and William, of blessed memory; to my cherished husband, Ravid; and to my precious daughter, Leila. I am grateful for all they have taught me about kindness, compassion, and unconditional love.

CONTENTS

CONTENTS

INTRODUCTION

At this moment, all over the country and, indeed, the world, there are parents and teachers who are struggling to raise or teach some very special children. These children may have been born with some condition, the cause of which is unknown, such as autism. They may have developed the condition as a result of experiences in the womb, as is the case with fetal alcohol effect. Or they may have acquired a condition, such as traumatic brain injury, in their early years of development. At times these children behave in ways that are worrisome and baffling to the adults who love them and want to help them learn. Many of these parents and teachers—and you may be one of them—find themselves using outdated tools that are both ineffective and often deeply unsatisfying.

Positive Discipline is not a cure for any of the conditions children with special needs might have been born with or contracted. It is an approach to child rearing and teaching that emphasizes helping children learn valuable social and life skills that will help them make responsible decisions that lead to a more productive and satisfying life. Unlike traditional approaches, which utilize punishments and rewards to teach, Positive Discipline promotes an entirely different set of tools. All of these tools, which are discussed in detail throughout this book, are grounded in mutual respect (that is, respect for both our children and ourselves), empathic understanding of the child's point of view, and effective communication that encourages children to learn to solve problems. It is an approach that has proved successful and, indeed, life changing for many parents and teachers. For parents and teachers of children with special needs, Positive

Discipline offers the same powerful perspectives and practices for helping children to lead happy and capable lives.

In this book we have sought to fill a gap in the literature of parenting and teaching children with special needs. Three things convince us that the time is right and the task is vital. First, we strongly believe that *all* children have the need to belong and feel significant in socially useful ways. Second, we have seen the wondrous results that come from treating children (with and without special needs) and ourselves with dignity and respect, using kindness and firmness at the same time, and trying to understand the beliefs behind their behaviors. Third, we have heard too often from parents and teachers with whom we've worked that, yes, Positive Discipline is a very compelling perspective, but it doesn't apply to *my* child or student because he or she has (fill in the special need). We want to reassure parents and teachers that Positive Discipline is indeed very helpful for their children with special needs.

We address parents and teachers of children from birth to around age eight. This is not because Positive Discipline does not apply to older children. Rather, it is to keep the scope of the book manageable.

As their children frequently stand out in some way, parents of children with special needs must also contend with the judgments of strangers, teachers, and even members of their own families. Much of the information and many of the suggestions they receive are about *managing* their children. Arlene and Steven had occasion to present some of their material on Positive Discipline for parents of children with autism at the yearly gathering of Positive Discipline certified practitioners. One of the participants was also the parent of a four-year-old boy on the autism spectrum. She approached them after the exercise and, eyes brimming with tears, said, "All the early intervention folks want me to just manage my son. You're telling me I get to raise him."

THE LAYOUT OF THE BOOK

Chapter 1 gives some brief background information about Positive Discipline, especially as it pertains to children with special needs both at home and in the classroom. In chapter 2 we present more detail on the Positive Discipline approach to understanding behavior, both "misbehavior" and "innocent behavior," as it pertains to children with special needs. Chapter 3 presents some useful information on the brain, with a focus on problem solving. In chapter 4 we discuss a concept called "positive time-out," a cornerstone of the nonpunitive and mutually respectful Positive Discipline philosophy. Chapters 5 through 12 will acquaint you with a framework, based on Alfred Adler's work, that is the foundation of the Positive Discipline approach. These chapters will take the core tools of Positive Discipline and discuss how they can be adapted for children with various special needs. Each of the chapters in this section revolves around the story of one child. The children described in these chapters are real children. In some cases we have modified identifying information to preserve the anonymity of both the children and their families. Chapter 13 is a comprehensive summary of the many tools used in Positive Discipline with clear information about how to adapt and enhance them to use with children with special needs.

A warning here: It simply is not possible to go into detail about any one condition to such an extent as to cover it fully. The whole book would then be about that condition. Rather, we intend to demonstrate how virtually any Positive Discipline tool for a child who is developing typically can be adapted to use with a child who has special needs. Adaptation means altering the "delivery system," i.e., how the tool is used with your child. The heart of the tool and its adherence to the values of Positive Discipline are unchanged.

We invite you to read on!

POSITIVE DISCIPLINE

FOR CHILDREN WITH SPECIAL NEEDS

"BUT MY CHILD
IS DIFFERENT!"

Around the beginning of the twentieth century, in Vienna, there was a psychiatrist, Alfred Adler, who was a contemporary and, for a short time, a colleague of Sigmund Freud. In groundbreaking work, Adler broke away from Freud and developed theories of human development that were later significantly enhanced by Rudolf Dreikurs. Positive Discipline is based on the theories and methods of Adler and Dreikurs.

Adler believed that the primary motivation of all human beings is to belong and feel significant, and that psychologically healthy people seek belonging and significance in socially useful ways. By "socially useful" we mean two things. First, we mean that a person's attempts to connect and be important invite a positive response from those around her. Second, we allude to a concept coined by Adler that he called *Gemeinschaftsgefühl,* sometimes translated as "social interest." Adler believed that mental health can be measured by the degree of an individual's positive

> A primary purpose of *behavior* is to achieve a sense of belonging and significance. All of us are constantly making decisions related to how we will achieve this.

contribution to his or her community. Thus, a primary purpose of *behavior* is to act on that motivation to achieve a sense of belonging and significance. Sometimes children (and adults) make "mistakes" about how to find belonging and significance and "misbehave."

All of us are constantly making decisions, conscious or unconscious, in our daily lives related to how we will achieve this sense of belonging. This process began the day we were born (and some believe in utero). These decisions play out in the context of the communities we find ourselves in from birth on: families, preschools, child care, classrooms, peer groups, work groups, and larger communities. It is crucial to understand that children with special needs also make decisions about how to find belonging and significance. These decisions may look different. If the children are pampered (a huge temptation for many parents of children with special needs), they may decide that they feel loved when others give them "special service" and may decide to use their special needs to gain a sense of belonging and significance. Thus parents and teachers miss opportunities to help their children make decisions that lead them to feel capable. Another possibility is that children with special needs may be neglected, which could similarly misinform their decisions about how to achieve belonging and significance.

Dreikurs noted that children can easily go about meeting their need to belong in misguided ways, referring to these ways as "mistaken goals of behavior" (which we will discuss in more detail in chapter 2). He pointed out that children are excellent perceivers and noticers; if you doubt this, take a walk around the block with a toddler and notice how long it takes as your toddler finds everything endlessly fascinating. However, children are notoriously poor interpreters of what they see. As they interact with the people in their world, children make decisions based on their understanding of events. These decisions, often based on misinterpretations, lead them to pursue belonging and significance in ways that befuddle and sometimes enrage the adults who love them.

Three-year-old Courtney has Down syndrome. She is play-ing with her mother when the phone rings. Her mother gets up to answer the phone and, as she is speaking, Courtney hurls herself at her mother's knees and cries piteously. The mother shushes Courtney, which is briefly successful, but a few moments later finds her knees under assault once again. This is a scene that has played out numerous times, and the mother is exasperated yet again. But she gets off the phone quickly, picks Courtney up, and resumes their play, a little resentfully.

What could possibly be going on for Courtney? She has been playing with her mother, who leaves the game when the phone rings. Courtney notices this, of course, but has learned to misinterpret it. She may believe that the phone is more important to her mother than she is. Why else would her mother leave? Of course this is not true. However, "truth" does not matter here. If Courtney believes that it's true, she might develop a mistaken belief about what she must do to feel a sense of belonging with her mother. (There is more on mistaken beliefs in chapter 2.) She might believe that she must be the center of her mother's attention in order to feel connected and important. And her mother might feel as though she is neglecting Courtney anytime she diverts her attention.

This scene can, and frequently does, play out in many homes, regardless of special-needs status. This is an important point because when Adler and Dreikurs suggested that all human beings are driven to belong and seek significance in socially useful ways, they did not mean *except for children with autism or cerebral palsy or Down syndrome or attention-deficit/hyperactivity disorder (ADHD) or developmental delays or any of the myriad conditions that we consider "special needs."* All children are apt to misinterpret their experiences and pursue mistaken goals. However, Adler understood that children's tendencies to make decisions based on their misinterpretations are exacerbated when one or more of the following is true:

1. They are pampered.
2. They are neglected.
3. They are handicapped. (Adler used this word before it became politically unacceptable.)

Children with special needs may be pampered. When pampering them, parents often underestimate their children's capabilities and use their condition as a justification for low expectations. These children may be clever enough to use their parents' sympathy to convince them that they are needier than may be the case.

Other children with special needs may be neglected because their parents are so discouraged that they give up and neglect their children emotionally if not physically. These children do not receive the guidance they need to learn to find belonging and significance in socially useful ways.

INNOCENT BEHAVIORS

As we shall see in later chapters, children with special needs can demonstrate behavior that is not socially directed but instead is "innocent," i.e., related to the child's special condition. For example, a child with Tourette's syndrome is more than likely not misbehaving when he makes unusual noises. This is usually an "innocent behavior" resulting from his condition.

How we respond to this behavior can determine whether or not it becomes mistaken-goal behavior. The child's special need does not make *all* of his behavior "innocent." As we will see in later chapters, children with special needs pursue mistaken goals as well. Differentiating between the two kinds of behaviors (innocent and mistaken goal) presents unique challenges to both parents and teachers. It is our intent to present Positive Discipline concepts and tools that will be useful to both.

THE LENS

Positive Discipline is certainly not a cure for any of the conditions mentioned above. However, since belonging and significance are so vital to a happy and fulfilling life, we must find ways to help *all* children achieve these. Parents of young children with special needs struggle with a host of extra tasks that must be juggled constantly. These tasks include all of those that any parent faces: getting kids up and out the door in the morning, getting them to sleep, dressing them, providing nourishing foods, managing potty learning (a much nicer way to think of potty "training"), finding child care, et cetera. They must add to these tasks the often complicated overlay of whatever their child's condition is. In addition, they often must get to doctor or clinic appointments and special education meetings while trying to figure out how they are going to ask for yet more time off from work or make it to their other child's soccer game.

In parenting classes for parents of children with special needs, we work hard to present Positive Discipline not as a cure but as a *lens* for parents to view their children (and themselves) differently. It can be said that these parents have two perspectives to overcome. The first is the traditional child-rearing perspective that holds that when children misbehave they must be punished in such a way that they learn not to repeat the misbehavior and that when they are "good" they must be rewarded to ensure that this good behavior will continue. The second view is perhaps the tougher to overcome for some parents. It suggests that because of the range of challenging behaviors children with disabilities can demonstrate, they do not have the same needs for belonging and significance as do other children. In the first class we hand out three-dimensional glasses to the parents as an experiential way to emphasize looking at their children's behaviors and their own responses to these behaviors differently.

Let us state it clearly: Children with special needs of any sort still have the same need to belong and feel significant in ways that invite positive responses from those around them. What is different is how we as parents and teachers must adapt our interactions with them to take their special needs into account without allowing these needs to block our vision of the children underneath.

EDUCATION

The parents of children with special needs have always known that their kids deserved the same love and attention as other children. They also have always known that their children deserved to be educated to the best of their abilities. As a society we have not always treated the education of children with special needs with the urgency it deserves.

In 1975, the United States Congress passed a landmark piece of legislation called the Education of All Handicapped Children Act, Public Law 94–142. Over the years the act has been amended and updated, and it is now called the Individuals with Disabilities Education Act (IDEA). In essence, the law of the land has begun to catch up with what parents have always known: Our children, *all our children*, must have their education taken seriously. The law guarantees all children with special needs the right to a "free and appropriate public education." It also guarantees parents of children with special needs the right to be involved in their children's education and to both advocate for them and be heard.

According to the U.S. Department of Education, in 1970 only one in five children with disabilities was being educated. Several states actually had laws *excluding* children with special needs from attending *public* schools. Many children were institutionalized and their education neglected. While those of us who work in special education are well aware of the sometimes overwhelming documentation requirements, it is a fact that since parents of children with special needs convinced Congress to enact the law, IDEA has been instrumental in changing how our society as a whole views these children.

Teachers in both special education and regular education are confronted with meeting the educational needs of children whose special needs represent a wide spectrum of conditions. Some of these children are in special education full-time, some in regular education full-time, many in some blend of the two. Something they all have in common is that when their behavior is not "socially useful," it interferes with their ability to glean as much from their academic experiences as they might otherwise. It is no exaggeration to say that teachers of children with special needs can feel very challenged by these behaviors.

> *Four-year-old Kaleb attends preschool at a local Head Start program. He has been found by the local early childhood special education (ECSE) agency to have developmental delays. Though obviously very bright, Kaleb struggles with the simplest expectations of a preschool classroom. He refuses to come to circle time, instead darting under the art easel. When encouraged to come out and find a seat with the group, he screams, "No!" and tells the teacher he wants to go outside immediately. When he is reassured that the group will go outside but that circle time will happen before that, he jumps up, runs to the center of the classroom, crosses his arms dramatically, and screams, "Fine!" He remains away from the circle.*

Schools of education across the country are addressing behavior challenges like these in their curricula for aspiring teachers. There are several different approaches offered. What they all have in common is that they view behaviors such as Kaleb's as obstacles that must be overcome in order for children to gain increased access to all of the positive educational experiences their schools provide. (We will return to Kaleb at the end of this chapter.) To understand behavior in the context of the classroom, many programs teach functional behavioral assessment, a tool that uses meticulous observation to determine what it might be that children like Kaleb are getting from their behavior or what they might be seeking to avoid by employing it. In addition, many behavioral approaches now taught in graduate schools of education, to their credit, are beginning to recognize the power of the relationship between teachers and students to help students develop the skills to manage their own behavior. And finally, well-researched systems such as Positive Behavioral Interventions and Supports have discovered that any system must be taught at least schoolwide (and preferably school-districtwide) and on a number of different levels, ranging from a general curriculum for most students to more specialized interventions for children whose behaviors present more significant challenges.

PARENTING AND TEACHING WITH A LONG-TERM VIEW

With this kind of preparation available to aspiring teachers, it is reasonable to wonder what Positive Discipline has to offer that is different and could enhance and deepen systems such as Positive Behavioral Interventions and Supports. To begin to answer this, let us perform an exercise together. Think of your child with special needs, your own child if you are a parent or a student you know if you are a teacher. Make a list of the behaviors that you find most challenging. If you are like the parents and teachers in our workshops, the list will look something like this:

- Screaming
- Hitting
- Tantrums
- Whining
- Demanding

- Odd fixations
- Disrupting the class
- Running away
- Hiding
- Refusal

For many groups, the list could go on and on. Now, indulge us for another moment. After you read this paragraph, put the book down and close your eyes. Imagine that you are sitting comfortably in your living room or classroom and thirty years have gone by. You hear a knock at the door. The door opens and in walks the child you had in mind when we made the list of challenging behaviors. This child is now grown up, somewhere between thirty and thirty-eight years old. What would you like to be true about this adult in your living room or classroom?

Again, if your answers are like those of groups in our workshops, the list will include things like:

- Confident
- Educated

- Respectful
- Independent

- Compassionate
- Healthy
- Sense of humor
- Good parent
- Working
- Likeable
- Honest
- Kind

(One of our favorite responses was from a dad who, when asked what he wanted to be true about his son thirty years later, replied, "Just visiting." What a wonderful way to describe independence!)

In adopting a Positive Discipline approach, we are taking a long-term view. We are concerned with the kinds of men, women, parents, and citizens our children will be. The behavioral approaches advocated in many parenting classes and taught in most schools of education will, in fact, work. *Yes, you read that correctly!* Rewards and punishments work. Systems built on stickers for good behavior and the loss of privileges for bad behavior all are effective in the short term. Positive Discipline—an authoritative approach built on a foundation of mutual respect, utilizing kindness and firmness at the same time, with an emphasis on problem solving and teaching valuable social and life skills—may not provide quick results, especially if you are using a very different style now. However, we believe it will lead to children developing the character traits and skills necessary for the second list you made above. Positive Discipline is supported by recent public-health research that has demonstrated that an authoritative approach to discipline leads children to develop greater responsibility over their lives and increased academic success.[1] It is also supported by research in the past two decades that affirms the importance of emotional connection between children and adults (parents *and* teachers) in optimal brain development.

Back in Kaleb's classroom, his teacher, using a technique from Positive Discipline, first asked herself how *she* was feeling about Kaleb's behavior, knowing that this was the clue to help her understand the belief behind it and, therefore, some possible solutions. She realized that she was annoyed that the behavior kept repeating and worried that Kaleb wasn't benefiting from the fun that the rest of the class was having at circle time. The teacher's emotional reaction was a powerful clue that Kaleb was pursuing the mistaken goal of "undue attention." (You will learn how to determine the mistaken goal in the next chapter.) Armed with this knowledge, she made a plan.

Before the next circle time she showed Kaleb a "first/then" sheet. On this sheet were two pictures: Under "first" there was a picture of children at circle time; under "then" was a picture of children playing outside. She also told him that she was really looking forward to playing hide-and-seek with him outside. At circle time, Kaleb was still antsy. The teacher saw him glance down repeatedly at the "first/then" sheet, but he stayed in the circle until it was time to go outside. The hide-and-seek game afterward was great fun!

It can be very encouraging to think of a behavior challenge as an opportunity to teach social and life skills that help your child grow into a capable, happy, contributing adult. Keep the end results in mind while enjoying your child now.

2

TRY THESE NEW LENSES!

Four-year-old Alan has extremely limited verbal language; he rarely interacts with other people except for his parents; he does not play with toys as do other children his age; and he shows alarm or upset when he hears certain environmental sounds or when people get too close to him. Alan's school district evaluation team determined that he meets the criteria for autism spectrum disorder and, with his parents, it was decided that his educational needs could be best met in an early childhood special education preschool located in his public elementary school. During his initial two weeks, upon arrival at the school Alan walked from the car to the building while holding his mother's hand. But then, as soon as he walked through the doorway of the school, he began to lean on his mother and then stopped walking. His mother verbally reminded him to walk while gently tugging him along. He often pulled his body in the opposite direction. Then he sat on the

floor of the school hallway and began tapping the floor re-
petitively with the palms of his hands. Some days, his mother
responded by picking him up and carrying him into his class-
room. Other days, she tried to help him walk by lifting him
to a standing position so that his feet could bear some weight
and then scooting him down the hallway into the classroom.
Most days, he passively allowed her to either carry him or
"walk" him. Occasionally, he used more physical effort to
pull away from her, scratched her arm, and then sat on the
floor while screaming and crying.

Is this behavior unique to a child with special needs? No. A situation like this, in which a child shows initial reluctance to begin a new school program, is common in early childhood settings, regardless of whether the child has a special need. A new classroom with unfamiliar people at the start of the school year might be a scary experience for any young child. Knowing very few people in the class, he might not feel a sense of belonging. Having spent little time in the classroom, any child initially might not understand its purpose nor feel a sense of significance while there. As a result, he may attempt to achieve belonging and significance in ways that are not socially useful.

When a child has a special need, the limitations associated with this condition (e.g., delays in communication, difficulties with processing information from his various senses, delays in cognition, et cetera) can lead to even greater levels of discomfort. The resulting behaviors may look exaggerated for two reasons. First, the child might have very appropriate fears about belonging and significance in this new and unfamiliar environment. Second, his ways of demonstrating discomfort may look unusual, even scary, to people around him (e.g., a child who does not speak might make loud noises, a child with a sensory-regulation impairment might move his body in ways that are not typical, a child who has trouble processing information might not respond quickly or might not seem to understand).

Positive Discipline's perspective on misguided behaviors is the same for children with special needs as for children without them: (1) Children have a need to belong and to feel significant. (2) A child who has a mistaken belief about how to achieve belonging and significance may decide to engage in behaviors that are not socially useful. (3) Understanding these mistaken beliefs allows parents and teachers to respond in helpful ways.

POSITIVE DISCIPLINE'S PERSPECTIVE

- Children need to belong and to feel significant.
- A mistaken belief about belonging and significance may lead a child to "misbehave."
- Understanding mistaken beliefs allows us to respond helpfully.

Furthermore, the Positive Discipline perspective sees each child as unique and valuable and takes into account both strengths and learning challenges. In the same way that we would encourage *any* parent or teacher to choose a Positive Discipline tool appropriate for the child and the situation, we encourage adaptation of the tools to make them useful and appropriate for children with special needs.

In this chapter, we will use examples to illustrate how behavior challenges of children with special needs can be viewed through the lens of Positive Discipline. Further, we will present the Mistaken Goal Chart, Positive Discipline's "road map" for (1) determining which mistaken belief is operating when a child with special needs behaves in ways that are not socially useful and (2) deciding what to do, both preventatively and in response to the misguided behavior. It is important for you, the parents and teachers of children with special needs, to understand that we determine the belief behind the child's behavior in exactly the same way we would for *any* child. In this respect, your child's special need is only one consideration, as *any* child can develop and exhibit a misguided behavior.

THE POSITIVE DISCIPLINE LENS

All Children Strive for Belonging and Significance

Does Alan, in the story above, have a need for belonging and significance? Some may say, "No, Alan does not have a need for belonging. He has autism!" and continue the perpetration of the myth that children with autism are incapable of intimate social relationships and don't demonstrate either a need to belong or a sense of belonging. Similarly, they may say, "No, Alan does not have a need for or sense of significance because his delays in developmental skills combined with his sensory impairment preclude his understanding of feeling significant."

Through the lens of Positive Discipline, we believe that Alan and all children with handicapping conditions, regardless of the type or degree of disability, have *a need for and a sense of belonging.* Especially among children who have difficulties with forming and maintaining relationships, belonging to a supportive, nurturing community is crucial.

Further, children who are significantly impacted by a condition that affects their ability to effectively interact with others *do* have a sense of belonging. We observe this, for example, when the young child with autism runs in the direction of his father (upon his father's arrival at school) and begins to jump, flap his arms, and make happy sounds, all the while not directly gazing at his father's face. This is apparent when the child with an anxiety disorder leans heavily into her mother when they visit the home of a neighbor. We see this when the child who is profoundly handicapped with multiple disabilities (visual impairment, orthopedic impairment, profound mental retardation) smiles when hearing her parent's voice or turns her head in the direction of her caregiver. Alan, in the above story, held his mother's hand, tugged against his mother, and allowed her to carry him or "walk" him down the hall. These are just small examples of the many ways that children with special needs show their sense of belonging.

We recognize that it can be hard for us to discern that a child's behaviors indicate the need for and sense of belonging. Yet the child's efforts to fulfill this need for an internal sense of belonging through his actions are unfaltering. As parents and teachers of these children, we must rise to the challenge of seeing the things they do as attempts to belong, as we would with any child. Then we must help them express these attempts in clearer and more socially useful ways.

Through the lens of Positive Discipline, we believe that Alan and all children with handicapping conditions, regardless of the type or degree of disability, have a need for and sense of significance. If provided with a method of choosing that is within their capabilities (e.g., using words, pointing to pictures, eye gazing or orienting the body to a desired item, et cetera), children with special needs usually respond accordingly, demonstrating which choices are meaningful and important to them. If offered something that is not to their liking, children with disabilities may use any number of means to refuse it (using words, crying, pushing away, moving away, closing their eyes, et cetera).

> We must rise to the challenge of seeing the things our children do as attempts to belong, as we would with any child.

Through making choices and by refusing items or activities, children with special needs communicate their need for and sense of significance. Their vocalizations or actions communicate, *I choose this thing because it is significant to me* or *I reject this thing because it is not significant to me.*

In the story about Alan, his need for and sense of significance is demonstrated when he stops at the doorway of the school, when he tugs against his mother, and when he allows his mother to carry him or "walk" him. There are many behaviors that children with special needs engage in to attempt to achieve significance. As you gain a heightened understanding of how your children demonstrate their need for and sense of significance, you can help them to acquire more socially useful ways of expressing themselves.

Mistaken Beliefs About Belonging and Significance Lead to Misguided Behavior

In order to understand how to help children with special needs who demonstrate challenges through their behaviors, we must first understand the underlying mistaken beliefs behind those behaviors. Often without their explicit awareness, our children are making decisions about themselves and their world and what they must do to thrive or survive in it. As we saw through the story about Courtney in chapter 1, these decisions can be made based on inaccurate interpretations about belonging and significance—in other words, on the basis of mistaken beliefs. When children act on mistaken beliefs by engaging in behaviors that are not socially useful, they are likely to invite unwelcome feelings in parents and teachers and may further provoke unwanted responses. An analysis of the Mistaken Goal Chart will help you gain clarity about the possible mistaken beliefs that underlie children's challenging behaviors.

As we can see from the chart, there are four mistaken beliefs that underlie the behaviors of children when that behavior is not socially useful (fifth column). Associated with each of the mistaken beliefs is a mistaken goal (first column) that a child, without explicit awareness, reveals through her misguided actions. Both the beliefs and related goals are considered *mistaken* because they lead her to make faulty attempts at achieving belonging and significance.

The adult's feelings about and reaction to the child's behavior (second and third columns) and the way the child responds to the adult's attempts to stop the behavior (fourth column) are clues to the mistaken goal of the child's behavior. By uncovering the mistaken goal, the adult can understand the mistaken belief behind the child's behavior, understand the "coded message" that is what the child really wants to communicate (sixth column), and replace the adult's own ineffective responses (third column) with proactive and encouraging responses (seventh column).

How will you know when the behaviors of your child with special needs are related to mistaken beliefs that lead to misguided attempts at achieving belonging and significance? The following examples will help.

Five-year-old Noah enjoyed circle time at the community preschool he attended. Although he had a history of developmental delay, especially in the area of communication, he frequently used the language he did have to make his needs and desires known and to express his opinions about things. At circle time each day, it was not unusual for him to loudly interrupt his teacher many times during the activity to request his favorite songs and stories or to express his dislike for what she had chosen. Feeling annoyed by Noah's repeated interruptions, his teacher gave him frequent reminders to keep his voice quiet when she or others were talking. He usually stopped for about a minute but then returned to interrupting. On some days, Noah was especially persistent in blurting out his thoughts and would stand up while talking in a tireless effort to get his teacher to listen to and respond to him.

What are some the clues in this scenario that help us understand the motivation underlying Noah's continual acts of interrupting during circle time? First, let's look at the teacher's responses: She *felt annoyed* and she gave him *frequent reminders* to remain quiet when people were talking. And what did Noah do in response to the reminders? He usually *stopped temporarily* but then *resumed* the unwanted verbalizations and then stood up while talking if the interruptions alone weren't successful. An examination of the second, third, and fourth columns of the Mistaken Goal Chart reveals that Noah mistakenly believes that he counts or belongs only when he's being noticed (fifth column), and the mistaken goal related to his actions is undue attention (first column). That is, the motivation underlying Noah's acts of interrupting is the mistaken belief that by getting undue attention, he will achieve a sense of belonging and significance. If Noah wore a shirt with his underlying message in bold letters that his teacher could see, it would read, "**Notice me! Involve me usefully.**"

To respond to Noah's underlying message, the teacher can invite him to choose a favorite song or story before circle time. During circle time, if Noah interrupts, the teacher can gently put her hand on Noah's shoulder while ignoring his outbursts. It may take a while for Noah to change

MISTAKEN GOAL CHART						
The child's goal is:	If the parent/ teacher feels:	And tends to react by:	And if the child's response is:	The belief behind the child's behavior is:	Coded messages	Parent/teacher proactive and encouraging responses include:
Undue Attention (to keep others busy or to get special service)	Annoyed Irritated Worried Guilty	Reminding Coaxing Doing things for the child he/she could do for him/ herself	Stops temporarily but later resumes same or another disturbing behavior	I count (belong) only when I'm being noticed or getting special service. I'm only important when I'm keeping you busy with me.	**Notice Me; Involve Me Usefully**	Redirect by involving child in a useful task to gain useful attention; say what you will do (Example: "I love you and will spend time with you later."); avoid special service; have faith in child to deal with feelings (don't fix or rescue); plan special time; help child create routine charts; engage child in problem solving; use family/ class meetings; set up nonverbal signals; ignore behavior with hand on shoulder.
Misguided Power (to be boss)	Challenged Threatened Defeated	Fighting Giving in Thinking *You can't get away with it* or *I'll make you* Wanting to be right	Intensifies behavior. Complies with defiance. Feels he/ she's won when parent/ teacher is upset even if he/she has to comply Passive power (says *yes* but doesn't follow through).	I belong only when I'm boss, in control, or proving no one can boss me. You can't make me.	**Let Me Help; Give Me Choices**	Redirect to positive power by asking for help; offer limited choices; don't fight and don't give in; withdraw from conflict; be firm and kind; act, don't talk; decide what you will do; let routines be the boss; leave and calm down; develop mutual respect; set a few reasonable limits; practice follow-through; use family/ class meetings.

The child's goal is:	If the parent/ teacher feels:	And tends to react by:	And if the child's response is:	The belief behind the child's behavior is:	Coded messages	Parent/teacher proactive and encouraging responses include:
Revenge (to get even)	Hurt Disappointed Disbelieving Disgusted	Hurting back Shaming Thinking *How could you do such a thing?*	Retaliates Intensifies Escalates the same behavior or chooses another weapon	I don't think I belong, so I'll hurt others as I feel hurt. I can't be liked or loved.	**I'm Hurting; Validate My Feelings**	Acknowledge hurt feelings; avoid feeling hurt; avoid punishment and retaliation; build trust; use reflective listening; share your feelings; make amends; show you care; act, don't talk; encourage strengths; don't take sides; use family/class meetings.
Assumed Inadequacy (to give up and be left alone)	Despairing Hopeless Helpless Inadequate	Giving up Doing things for the child that he/she could do for him/herself Overhelping	Retreats further Becomes passive Shows no improvement Is not responsive	I can't belong because I'm not perfect, so I'll convince others not to expect anything of me; I am helpless and unable; it's no use trying because I won't do it right.	**Don't Give Up on Me; Show Me a Small Step**	Break task down into small steps; stop all criticism; encourage any positive attempt; have faith in child's abilities; focus on assets; don't pity; don't give up; set up opportunities for success; teach skills/ show how, but don't do for; enjoy the child; build on his/her interests; use family/ class meetings.

his behavior, but it will be easier for the teacher to follow through with ignoring the "misbehavior" when she knows that she has given Noah appropriate attention while having patience and faith in Noah to eventually learn what works and what doesn't work.

Six-year-old Rebecca enjoys collecting small horse figures. This interest began two years ago when she was in preschool and her class went on a field trip to a local farm. On route from the farm, Rebecca's mother stopped at a nearby market. While her mother gathered a few groceries for dinner, Rebecca discovered the horse and stable play set near the checkout stand. When her mother began to check out with groceries, Rebecca put several toy horses on the conveyor belt. Her mother spoke while signing to Rebecca, explaining to her hearing-impaired daughter that only groceries would be purchased today.

Rebecca refused to return the horses to the shelf and instead held them on the conveyer belt. Feeling challenged by Rebecca's lack of cooperation, her mother quickly walked Rebecca back to the shelf and forced her to put the horses back. As her mother returned to the checkout counter, Rebecca grabbed the horses and ran with them to a nearby aisle where her mother could see her but could not get to her easily. Her mother told her, now in a louder voice while signing, to return the horses to the shelf. Rebecca held the horses close to her chest and didn't move. Not wanting to create a scene in the market, Rebecca's mother told her that she would buy her one horse. Rebecca dropped two of the horses and brought one with her to the checkout stand. Since that day, Rebecca's mother buys her a small horse whenever they shop together at a store that carries this favorite toy. Her collection now exceeds a hundred horses!

Let's examine some of the clues that help us understand the motivation underlying Rebecca's undesirable actions. Her mother was feeling *challenged* by Rebecca's lack of cooperation. Further, she demanded that Rebecca follow directions by *forcing her* to put the horses back. Rebecca, in response, *intensified her behavior* by grabbing and running with the horses. Her mother *gave in* by letting Rebecca have one of the horses, and Rebecca *complied with defiance* when she dropped two of the horses.

It certainly looks as if Rebecca is acting out of the mistaken belief that she counts or belongs only when she is in control and proving that her mother can't boss her. If this is the case, Rebecca's mistaken goal is misguided power. Rebecca's sense of belonging and significance are achieved when she acts in ways that lead her to feel in control and powerful, even when these actions greatly reduce the pleasure of a mother-daughter outing. If Rebecca wore a shirt with her underlying message, it would read, **"Let me help. Give me choices!"**

If Rebecca's mother had responded to the message on the shirt she might have handled the situation by giving her child the following choice: "I need your help to save money to buy the horses. Do you want to save your money to buy one horse or three horses? How long do you think it will take? You decide." It is very likely that Rebecca would have made a choice because she would have felt empowered by having a choice.

Jasmine was a very busy student in her second-grade classroom. Although she was performing at grade level in all her subjects, her impulsive actions and verbalizations during class, combined with her constant movement (up and out of her seat frequently or rocking back in her chair to the point of falling over occasionally), led her teacher to send her to the office on a daily basis. At the school office, Jasmine reported to the vice principal, who lectured her about classroom behavior expectations.

What concerned her parents and teachers the most were her disrespectful interactions with a new student in the classroom. For example, upon returning from the school office one day, Jasmine, while sitting at her desk, put her foot out in the aisle as her classmate was walking by. The girl tripped and fell to the floor, bruising the palms of her hands and breaking her glasses. Jasmine's teacher was shocked and upset that Jasmine would behave that way toward the new classmate. She sent her back to the school office and told her that she might be suspended from school for a few days.

When Jasmine returned to the classroom after another focused lecture from the vice principal, she was observed whittling a hole in her desk surface using the tip of her pen. On the initiative of her parents, Jasmine was eventually referred for a multidisciplinary team evaluation that determined that she had attention-deficit/hyperactivity disorder.

This story clearly demonstrates how *a misbehaving child is a discouraged child.* Let's look at this story within the framework of the Mistaken Goal Chart to understand Jasmine's behaviors through the lens of Positive Discipline. Jasmine's thoughtless act toward her classmate invited feelings of *disappointment and disbelief* from her teacher. Her teacher reacted to Jasmine by sending her back to the school office and added a little more "bite" to this punishment by *threatening* her potential suspension from school. Upon her return, Jasmine *chose another "weapon"* by *damaging school property.* An analysis of this situation leads us to conclude that Jasmine's sense of belonging was greatly compromised by the punishment she faced on a daily basis: removal from her class. It's not surprising that she would have the mistaken belief "I don't belong, so I'll hurt others as I feel hurt." The mistaken goal of revenge was the driving force behind her misguided actions. If Jasmine wore a shirt with her underlying message, it would read, **"I'm hurting; validate my feelings."**

If the teacher and vice principal understood Jasmine's mistaken goal, they could stop the revenge cycle by guessing what Jasmine felt hurt about and validating her feelings. Children who have the mistaken goal of revenge usually feel encouraged when their feelings are validated. Jasmine might then be willing to work on a solution that would work for her to stay in her seat. When the revenge cycle was broken, she would likely not hurt others. If she did, it would still be most effective to validate feelings and then work on solutions with all the children involved.

Six-year-old Joshua has a significant speech and communication delay that was discovered when he was two years old. While he understands most of what is said to him, his expressive language is noticeably behind that of other children his age. As he struggles to clearly express his thoughts in complete

sentences, he seems to be aware that his classmates cannot al-
ways understand his misarticulated words.

In the first month of school, during group discussions in his
first-grade class, his teacher often felt inadequate in her abil-
ity to engage Joshua. He did not volunteer, and whenever she
called on him to share with the group, he moved back in his
chair, looked down, and did not speak. After several weeks
like this, Joshua's teacher requested that he be considered for
a special education classroom placement because she had lit-
tle hope that including him in a regular class setting would be
helpful for him.

Very discouraged by his communication difficulties, Joshua was *pas-sive and unresponsive* to his teacher's efforts to invite his participation. His teacher *felt inadequate and hopeless* and eventually *gave up* on him, thinking that a different class placement would be better for him than his mainstream classroom setting. An examination of the Mistaken Goal Chart suggests that Joshua's mistaken belief is that he can't belong and he is unable to adequately participate with his classmates. Joshua was operating from the mistaken goal of assumed inadequacy. If he wore a shirt with his underlying message, it would read, **"Don't give up on me!"** and **"Show me a small step."**

A teacher who understood the mistaken goal of assumed inadequacy would make every effort to focus on small steps that would help Joshua feel encouraged and give up his belief that he is inadequate. First, she could set up opportunities for Joshua and his classmates to feel successful by having the children in the class pair up with one another to talk about specific discussion questions. Then she could have all the children return to the large group to share what they learned, while sitting next to their partners. The success that Joshua experienced working one on one with a partner could boost his feelings of belonging and significance and improve his confidence to speak up in the group.

In the later chapters of this book, we will describe some invaluable

Positive Discipline tools, the Parent/Teacher Proactive and Encouraging Responses (seventh column), that we can use when our children with special needs act in misguided ways. These tools will help children replace their behaviors associated with the mistaken goals of undue attention, misguided power, revenge, and assumed inadequacy with behaviors that will, in the long term, help them to achieve and maintain a true sense of belonging and significance in their families and communities.

Some Innocent Behaviors May Be Disguised as Misbehavior! How Can We Tell?

In our initial analysis to understand the underlying belief behind the challenging behavior of children with special needs, one of the most important questions to ask about the behavior that concerns you is *not* "Is this behavior socially useful?" The likelihood is that it is not, and that's why it concerns you. More important, you can ask initially, "Is this a socially motivated behavior?" which in Positive Discipline terms means, "Does this behavior arise from the child's mistaken belief about belonging and significance?"

In our earlier example of Alan, we saw that he demonstrated a number of behaviors that are not socially useful and that could be examined for their social motivation. To consider which behaviors are socially motivated and associated with mistaken beliefs related to belonging and significance, it's helpful to list the sequence of his behaviors and to inspect each one individually. Here's what Alan did that was not socially useful:

- He leaned on his mother at the doorway and stopped walking.
- He pulled away from his mother.
- He sat on the floor of the school hallway.
- He tapped the floor repetitively with the palms of his hands.
- He passively allowed his mother to move him to his classroom.
- He used more physical effort to pull away from her.

- He scratched his mother.

- He sat in the hallway while screaming and crying.

Which of these behaviors is socially motivated and therefore related to Alan's mistaken beliefs about belonging and significance? To answer this question, let's refer back to the Mistaken Goal Chart. A clear understanding of this chart will greatly assist us in determining at what point Alan's behaviors became socially motivated problems.

For our current scrutiny of Alan's behaviors, let's focus on the second column, showing the adult's feeling, the fifth column, showing the belief behind the child's behavior, and the first column, showing the child's goal. The underlying mistaken belief related to each of the behaviors that Alan engaged in (listed above) is related to the feelings that the behavior invited in his mother. Through conversations with Alan's mother, his teacher noted that Alan's mother's feelings were as follows:

- He leaned on his mother at the doorway and stopped walking: neutral.

- He pulled away from his mother: mildly annoyed.

- He sat on the floor of the school hallway: worried.

- He tapped the floor repetitively with the palms of his hands: neutral.

- He passively allowed his mother to move him to his classroom: guilty.

- He used more physical effort to pull away from her: challenged.

- He scratched his mother: disbelieving.

- He sat in the hallway while screaming and crying: helpless.

So let's return to the earlier question: Which of Alan's behaviors are socially motivated and therefore related to his mistaken beliefs about belonging and significance? By his mother's feelings associated with each of the behaviors, we see that the following behaviors were socially motivated and therefore related to mistaken goals:

- He pulled away from his mother: undue attention.

- He sat on the floor of the school hallway: undue attention.

- He passively allowed his mother to move him to his classroom: undue attention.

- He used more physical effort to pull away from her: misguided power.

- He scratched his mother: revenge.

- He sat in the hallway while screaming and crying: assumed inadequacy.

What about Alan's first behavior, which did not arouse feelings in his mother: leaning on her at the doorway and stopping his forward movement. It certainly was not socially useful that he did this because it was unhelpful to his mother, who was trying to smoothly transition him to his classroom. However, because uncomfortable feelings were not aroused in her and she remained neutral in her interactions with him, this is not considered a socially motivated behavior. So what was the motivation for his leaning and stopping? Likely, given what we know about the sensory-processing challenges of children with autism, Alan's leaning and stopping were his innocent responses to the overwhelming stimuli in the school hallway that he was not accustomed to: the bright, colorful posters on the doors and walls in the entryway, the rush of children and parents moving past him, the lighting in the hallway, the smells from inside the school building, the sounds from voices and from the air-conditioning system, et cetera.

Alan's mother knows that new environments are difficult for him at first, so his leaning on her when he initially entered did not invite uncomfortable feelings in her. However, what if she did not know that his compromised sensory system leads him to experience difficulty with entering new settings? What if she had become annoyed or worried or challenged by his leaning and stopping, believing he was "doing this on purpose," and then demonstrated her feeling and belief by raising her voice or nagging or threatening? His behaviors that are *socially neutral* (innocent behaviors) because they are associated with his disability and not related to his sense of belonging and significance would have been at risk of becoming socially motivated problems.

Now let's consider Alan's other behavior that did not invite an uncomfortable emotional response in his mother: tapping the floor repetitively with the palms of his hands. This also is an innocent behavior that is not socially motivated. Alan's mother understands that tapping things is one of the repetitive behaviors that Alan frequently displays that is associated with his autism. If Alan's mother had misinterpreted the behavior and instead had reacted to him in negative ways while feeling annoyed, worried, challenged, angry, disappointed, disbelieving, despairing, or inadequate, his innocent tapping might have become socially directed. For example, if his mother had tried to *make* him stop, he might have continued tapping with greater intensity, demonstrating the mistaken goal of misguided power and believing, *I belong when I'm in control. You can't make me stop!* Because his mother remained neutral in her feelings and responses, Alan's tapping did not intensify and remained socially neutral.

If parents and teachers misunderstand the atypical behaviors of children with special needs, those innocent behaviors that are associated with their handicapping conditions (e.g., repetitive behaviors in children with autism, tics in children with Tourette's syndrome, slower response time in children with cognitive delays, impulsive behaviors in children with ADHD, et cetera), they may unintentionally respond to children *as if* their behaviors are socially motivated, *as if* there is mischievous social intent leading to the behaviors. When socially neutral behaviors are misunderstood, children may come to mistakenly believe that belonging and significance are achieved when they engage in behaviors associated with their particular condition.

In the story about Alan, his mom wanted to help him enter the school with more independence and greater ease. She decided to arrive fifteen minutes later each school day so as to avoid all the noise and activity at the entryway of the school when other children were arriving. She felt empowered as she practiced Positive Discipline tools that allowed her to teach Alan how to stay calm in this difficult situation. She demonstrated patience as she decided what *she* would do: walk slowly toward the classroom, literally *taking small steps,* while allowing Alan time to have his feelings and to process all the sensory information. She was kind and firm, stopping when he stopped and moving when he was ready to move. She didn't "fight him" and she didn't give in. She remained quiet except to occasionally validate his feelings as he worked out how to transition into the school environment. In a mutually respectful fashion, she used their daily arrival at school as time for training about self-management and autonomy.

The following is a summary of the steps to initially follow when helping children with special needs:

1. List the behaviors of concern.

2. Investigate with the adult interacting with the child what feelings and reactions are invited by each of the behaviors.

3. Based on the feelings and reactions of the adult, and the responses of the child, determine what mistaken beliefs and mistaken goals are associated with each of the behaviors.

4. For those behaviors that are innocent because they are associated with the child's handicapping condition and not socially motivated, provide appropriate treatment or instruction to reduce the problem. For example, occupational therapists skilled in evaluating the sensory needs of a child with autism may recommend that parents and teachers carry out a regular *sensory diet* that is designed to reduce the child's self-stimulatory behaviors. Tactile activities, such as playing with a variety of textures (play dough, finger paints, sand, et cetera),

and vestibular and proprioceptive activities that involve movement, balance, and body awareness (swinging, running, bouncing on a therapy ball, jumping on a mini trampoline, et cetera) might be included in a child's unique sensory diet. (Positive Discipline tools can be used here as well.)

5. For the challenging behaviors that are associated with mistaken beliefs, use Positive Discipline tools to develop an individually tailored plan of prevention and response that will help the child to use more socially useful behaviors.

INNOCENT BEHAVIOR	MISTAKEN GOAL BEHAVIOR
• Teach skills • Provide therapy	• Determine mistaken belief behind the behavior
Use Positive Discipline Tools	

In later chapters of this book, the Positive Discipline tools used with children with special needs—for both prevention and intervention—will be described in detail. Examples of how to modify and adapt these tools will also be presented.

3

UNDERSTANDING THE BRAIN—YOURS AND THEIRS

Anthony Martin woke up late one morning and realized that if he didn't hurry, he would be late for work. Again! He groaned inwardly because he knew that getting his daughter Emily out the door in a hurry could be a recipe for disaster. Emily was six years old and had autism spectrum disorder. Although her year in kindergarten had been relatively successful, changes in her routine could still send her into a downward spiral of screaming rage and frustration.

Anthony hurried Emily through her morning routine, though he did remember to use the visual schedule that helped anchor Emily. Breakfast was tense, but Emily seemed to be rising to the occasion; Anthony was grateful. Emily got herself dressed, a fairly new skill of which both she and Anthony were justifiably proud.

Anthony looked at his watch. If traffic cooperated he might actually get Emily to child care in time for her to catch her bus to school and for him to get to work on time. Emily was humming as they left their apartment and walked down to the parking lot to get in the car. She stopped humming when Anthony passed the space that his car was assigned to. Emily expected the family car to be in it. However, because someone had been in his space when he returned from a trip to the market the night before, Anthony had parked across from it, meaning to go out later and move the car back to its usual spot.

Anthony led Emily across the parking lot to their car. Emily backed away from the car and started to intone, "No, no, no, no, no!" Anthony tried to reassure her that it was still their car and to gently guide her toward it. In an instant, Emily panicked and began slapping both at the air and at Anthony. She was now screaming, "NO! NO! NO!" Frustrated and realizing that he would be late, Anthony grabbed Emily by the shoulders and shook her, yelling, "Emily, this is our car! Get in the car!" Emily dissolved in tears and fell to the ground. Anthony picked her up (a little roughly) and maneuvered her into the car seat with great difficulty. Emily did not stop screaming or crying. Anthony felt ashamed.

What happened that morning at the Martins' is not uncommon in families with and without children with disabilities. Children do not always see the same need to hurry that their parents do. There is another common thread that runs through episodes such as this one. It has to do with what happens in our brains when we are under stress.

OUR BRAINS: THEN AND NOW

Thousands of years ago the world was a very different place. Our needs were different, and simpler as well. It was a world filled with danger, and humans had to react quickly to avoid animal predators, other humans wishing to do them harm, and the hardships of a frequently hostile environment. Our brains were well adapted to cope with these kinds of situations. They quickly sized up what confronted us and made one of three kinds of decisions. If possible, we ran to avoid the danger (flight). If necessary, we prepared to do battle (fight). At times, we kept ourselves rigidly still to avoid detection (freeze).

For millennia the way we used our brains was adequate for our needs. Over time, as our lives grew more complex, our need to reason and not just react grew stronger; we began to rely increasingly on a different area of the brain. The quickly reactive part of the brain, on which we depended for thousands of years, still serves us well (and sometimes gets us into trouble—more about that later), but we are no longer dependent solely on it for our survival.

Broadly speaking, our brains are made up of three parts. The brain stem is the most ancient and primitive part of the brain and is responsible for those survival responses (fight, flight, or freeze) mentioned above. The second part, also quite old, is the limbic system. Together, the brain stem and the limbic system are responsible for, among other things, how we feel about experiences and what sense we make of them, as well as for those survival responses. The third part of the brain is the cortex. While the workings of the cortex are complex, for our purposes here it is the part of the brain responsible for, again among other things, insight, flexibility of responses, and empathy, the ability to see things from someone else's perspective.

> When we are at our best, the parts of our brain work together well. There is a flow of energy and information among the three parts that allows us to deal with whatever experiences come our way.

When we are at our best, these parts of our brain work together well. There is a flow of energy and information among the three parts that allows us to deal with whatever experiences come our way. The primitive areas of our brain, the brain stem and the limbic system, might be considered our "first responders." They give us a preliminary read on an experience. But by themselves they can respond only with fight, flight, or freeze. However, with input from the cortex, we are able to make more measured and thoughtful responses. This is called executive functioning. Executive functioning is our ability to give thought to the experiences we are having, to consider a variety of responses, and to choose the one that makes the most sense to us. It is also through the cortex that we maintain an emotional connection with our children. As we saw at the Martins' home, the communication between the different parts of our brain is not always seamless.

To get a sense of how this works, let us go back to the image of the "first responders." In the role of first responders, the brain stem and limbic system (a part of which is called the amygdala) assess our experiences. Out of this assessment comes an initial determination as to how we feel about them, as well as a preliminary recommendation of how to respond. This information is communicated to the cortex, which adds its own contribution by analyzing it and applying insight, flexibility, and empathy to the decision-making process. Most experiences are easily processed using this system of shared responsibility. However, at times, the level of feeling in the amygdala and the urgency of the "fight, flight, or freeze" response overwhelm the cortex. When this happens, there is no insight, flexibility, or empathy added to the decision-making mix. At this point, executive functioning is effectively off-line and unavailable. Practically speaking, this means we are unable to engage in any kind of meaningful problem solving.

BRAIN IN THE PALM OF YOUR HAND

In their book, *Parenting from the Inside Out*,[2] Daniel Siegel and Mary Hartzell present an elegant and refreshingly (to us non–brain scientists) understandable explanation of the brain processes we described above. In our classes with both parents and teachers of children with and without special needs, this model remains one of the most useful and remembered tools. It's called "Brain in the Palm of Your Hand." What follows is a simplified version of Siegel and Hartzell's model.

If you hold up your hand in a fist with your four fingers curled over your thumb and your fingers facing you, this makes what Siegel calls "a surprisingly accurate general model of the brain" (figure 1). Your wrist is the spine. The center of your palm is the brain stem, the point at which the brain connects with the spine. Your thumb represents the limbic system as a whole and specifically the amygdala. The back of your hand represents the cortex as a whole; your curled fingers, and specifically your fingernails, represent the prefrontal section of the cortex.

When experiences do not create unmanageable stress, the prefrontal cortex smoothly exercises the process we call executive functioning. This is represented by the closed fist, as described above. To represent what happens when your amygdala is overwhelmed, keep your thumb curled and extend your fingers straight up (figure 2). Siegel and Hartzell refer to this process as "flipping your lid." Now imagine that, in reaction to your child or one of your students flipping his lid, you respond angrily without thinking. To picture this, hold up both hands with thumbs curled in, fingers extended upward, and palms facing each other (figure 3). With two flipped lids face to face (yours and your child's), how much helpful problem solving do you think is happening? (To watch a demonstration, go to www.youtube.com, type in "Daniel Siegel," and click on "Dr. Daniel Siegel presenting a hand model of the brain.")

Look again at your closed fist. Notice how your fingers, which represent the prefrontal cortex (executive functioning, flexible thinking, and empathy), curl around and contain your palm and thumb, which represent the brain stem and the limbic system (fight-flight-freeze response). For the most part, even when we are agitated, the prefrontal cortex does indeed do a good job wrapping up and containing (i.e., "keeping the lid on") the less rational and more reactive brain stem and limbic system. When we have flipped our lids, the fingers are uncurled and, suddenly,

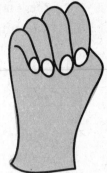

Figure 1. A model of the brain.

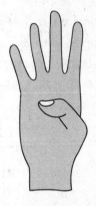

Figure 2. Flipping your lid.

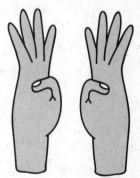

Figure 3. Two flipped lids trying to solve a problem.

there is nothing to contain the amygdala. There is no prefrontal cortex operating to think flexibly and override our fight-flight-freeze instinct.

Lois Ingber, a certified Positive Discipline trainer in San Diego, relates the story of one parent's remarkable extension of this image. This parent pointed out that when we make a fist in anger, the reverse is true. The thumb is on the outside of the fingers; it is the limbic system that is containing and overriding the prefrontal cortex.

One more aspect of the brain rounds out the picture even more. Siegel and Hartzell describe what are called mirror neurons. As human beings we are hardwired to connect with other human beings. From the very beginning of our lives we notice intently how other people look and, from our observations, the mirror neurons in our brains assess their mental and emotional states. This assessment, then, is a strong influence on how we react. Thus, in the example above, when a child flips her lid, a calm reaction on our part can act as a powerful brake on our child's runaway emotions as our mirror neurons "talk" to hers.

> When a child "flips her lid," a calm reaction on our part can act as a powerful brake on our child's runaway emotions as our mirror neurons "talk" to hers.

Let's go back to the example of Anthony and Emily Martin. On seeing her family's car so dramatically out of place, especially after working so diligently to stay on task despite feeling rushed, Emily's ability to be flexible was gone. Her amygdala was overwhelmed by the stress and she began to flip her lid by flapping her hands in the air and screaming, "No!" Her father had also worked diligently and thoughtfully to help Emily move more quickly on a morning when he felt like he simply could not be late for work. When Emily began flipping her lid, Anthony's emotional reserves were also depleted, and he reacted to Emily's distress by flipping his own lid, yelling at her and handling her somewhat roughly.

HIGH ROAD, LOW ROAD

Siegel and Hartzell use another image that we have found extremely helpful in our classes. They refer to the two kinds of responses we described above as either "high-road processing" or "low-road processing." High-road processing uses the prefrontal cortex and enables us to consider various ways of responding and the likely consequences of each way. We can choose the option that feels appropriate for the needs of the situation and maintains a positive emotional connection with our children. Low-road processing occurs when we have flipped our lids and reacted impulsively and, often, angrily. These are the responses we end up feeling bad about because we sense, usually correctly, that we have, according to Siegel and Hartzell, "behave[d] in ways that are frightening and confusing" to our children. It is also called "knowing better but not doing better"—a common plight of all parents. Understanding your brain can help, if not to change your reaction in the moment, at least to allow you to make amends when you have calmed down.

> Low-road processing occurs when we have "flipped our lids" and reacted impulsively and, often, angrily.

In Anthony Martin's situation, he knew almost immediately that Emily was already fragile from being rushed and that she was further thrown off course by the family car being, in her mind, significantly out of place. One possible high-road response would have been to make an empathetic statement to Emily, one that reflected that Anthony understood Emily's distress. For example, he might have gotten down to Emily's level, hugged her gently, and said, "Oh, Emily. You're upset that the car is in the wrong place." The communication to Emily that her father understood her and saw the world through her eyes might not have been a magical solution, but it could have set the stage for better problem solving.

At this point you might be thinking, *Well, sure! Anyone can come up with a better idea after the fact.* And, of course, you would be correct. Our point is not to imply in any way that any of us is on the high road all of the time. On the contrary, even though virtually all parents and teachers aspire to be on the high road, i.e., to respond to children thoughtfully and collaboratively, we all flip our lids and end up on the low road more often than we would like. Since this seems to be an unchanging truth of both parenting and teaching, what can we do?

The first thing we can do is to cultivate the ability to reflect about ourselves. Self-reflection entails being able to examine what we have said and done and decide whether we have acted in a way that is consistent with our values. When we can do this, we are more likely to increase the amount of time we spend on the high road. Please note that we said "increase"; we can't stress enough that it isn't realistic to think any of us can be there all of the time. In fact, we might argue that without our children and students occasionally being witnesses to adults' "blowing it," they might not learn to profit from their own mistakes. (More on mistakes later.)

After we have reflected, then what?

THE THREE *R*s OF RECOVERY

Once we have calmed down and given some thought to interactions with our children in which we were not at our best, there are three steps that will help us recover. Some refer to this calming process as "regathering" and consider it the fourth *R* of recovery.

THE THREE *R*s OF RECOVERY

1. Recognize
2. Reconcile
3. Resolve

Recognize: First, before anything else can happen, we must recognize that we have made a mistake. In Anthony Martin's case, after giving the matter some thought, he realized that Emily's initial reaction to the car being out of place was not a conscious attempt to make him angry or late. Emily was responding the way many children with autism spectrum disorder respond when they are used to a very specific routine and that routine is derailed. Once he was able to recognize that his mistake was having taken Emily's reaction personally, Anthony was able to move off the low road and on to the next step.

Reconcile: When we have made a mistake, and especially when the mistake has involved low-road behavior on our part, it is very important and helpful to make a sincere apology. For some parents and teachers, this can be a surprisingly difficult step to take. Some of us cannot remember adults ever apologizing to us as children. As a result, we might have developed the mistaken belief that adults' apologizing to children somehow undermines their authority. Others, especially some teachers, may have been taught to "never let them see you sweat," as if an apology were a sign of weakness.

On the contrary, a sincere apology has the capacity to undo some of the fear and confusion that our low-road behavior has engendered in our children. We want to stress the word *sincere* here, as there are some kinds of apologies that are not helpful. A sincere apology involves taking full responsibility (without guilt or shame) for what you have done. That responsibility can be returned in an underhanded way if you qualify your responses. Thus, "I'm really sorry that I yelled at you, but you weren't following the rules" gives with one hand and takes away with the other.

In the scenario with the Martins, Anthony reflected on his low-road behavior as he and Emily drove to her child care. As he did so, Emily continued to sniffle in the backseat. When they arrived Anthony gently got Emily out of the car seat. When she stepped out of the car, he knelt in front of her and said, "Emily, I'm so sorry I yelled at you and put you in your car seat so roughly. I should not have done that." Emily did not reply, but she maintained eye contact with Anthony for several seconds and stopped sniffling. Anthony smiled at her and held out his arms. Emily let herself be hugged and put her head on Anthony's shoulder. The Martins were now able to move on to the third step in recovery.

Resolve: Resolving involves coming up with a way to correct the mistake, to fix the problem. And helping our children learn problem solving is one of the greatest gifts we can give them. Without the ability to solve problems, children will be more easily overwhelmed by circumstances and will flip their lids more often. While this ability is vital at home, it is perhaps even more so at school and in the community. Children who can't solve problems will more than likely have a very difficult time at school. They will also be at risk for being unable to create and sustain positive relationships with other children.

> Helping our children learn problem solving is one of the greatest gifts we can give them.

In our society, we talk the talk about making mistakes. We tell children, "Everybody makes mistakes." But all too frequently we do not walk the walk. Think about mistakes that happen in the news. When is the last time you heard a public figure say something like, "Oops. That was a mistake. Here's how I plan to correct it"? Think further about the frequent public reaction to mistakes. Often we read or hear about a clamor for punishment, and there is speculation about who is going to lose their job as a result of a mistake. This way of looking at mistakes does not go unnoticed by our children. Despite what we might tell them, if we demonstrate that mistakes are unforgivable and, worse, unfixable, it should come as no surprise that this is how children will also come to view mistakes.

> If we demonstrate that mistakes are unforgivable and, worse, unfixable, it should come as no surprise that this is how children will also come to view mistakes.

Thus, teaching children how to solve problems and fix mistakes is crucial. There is no better way to start teaching than to demonstrate the skill when (not *if*) we make mistakes. Anthony Martin realized this once his "lid" was firmly back in place. He understood that he needed not only to own responsibility for what he had done but also to use this opportunity to help Emily learn about fixing mistakes. Anthony's challenge in doing this was that Emily's condition, autism spectrum disorder, made communication with her more difficult. Then he remembered the communication notebook that Emily's teachers had made for him to use with her. The notebook contained a variety of picture symbols that, when paired with saying the words out loud, helped Emily understand things better. (We will talk more in later chapters about picture symbols and other adaptations for children with special needs.)

When Anthony and Emily got to her child care, despite already being late, Anthony took an extra couple of minutes to sit with Emily and her communication notebook. Using the picture symbols, Anthony pointed out how Emily had been feeling (worried because their car was out of place) and what he had done (get angry). He apologized again and then pointed to a picture that represented "helping." He said, "Next time, I'll help you when you're worried. No yelling." Emily repeated, "No yelling."

Later, Anthony remembered other tools Emily's teacher had given him. They included a "social story"[3] about how Emily could cope when something unexpected occurred and a choice wheel to help Emily identify and choose a different response when she was worried. For now, however, Anthony felt proud that he had been able to make amends with Emily after flipping his lid. His understanding of the brain and the skills he had learned about recovery from mistakes provided a foundation for his success.

4

POSITIVE TIME-OUT

Things were not going well for the State University Tigers on the basketball court. They were trailing by sixteen points with only four minutes left in the game. Their coach was angrily pacing the sideline, slapping his leg with a rolled-up program. At one point he stopped pacing and screamed at one of his players to call a time-out. Because of the roar of the crowd, the player did not immediately hear him. The coach screamed louder and made his hands into a T, the universal symbol for a time-out. The player signaled to the referee and time was called. The players approached their bench warily; they could almost see the smoke coming out of the coach's ears.

When his team arrived at the bench, the coach coldly pointed at the bench for the players to sit down. The players sneaked looks at one another. Their coach's fury was obvious. When the team was seated, the coach said, "This has been the worst display of basketball I have ever seen in all my years of coaching!

Were ANY of you listening when we went over the game plan?" He paused, as if waiting for an answer. No one replied. "Well?!" he prompted. The players all looked down at the floor.

"Answer me!" the coach screamed. Still no one said a word. He pointed to the team's center and said, "Are you TOTALLY incapable of stopping your man? He has blown by you every time he has the ball. Did someone PAY you to play so poorly?" When the center looked shocked but did not reply, the coach pointed to the end of the bench and said furiously, "Go. Sit away from us. And you THINK about what you need to do to stop your man from scoring every time he has the ball." The center looked and felt ashamed. He shuffled to the end of the bench, almost in tears, and sat down. He felt as though he had completely let his team down and didn't deserve to be a starting player.

"And YOU!" The coach was now pointing at the team's point guard. "You're supposed to be running the show out there. Do you not understand what 'running the show' means? Do I have to draw you a picture?! When we needed to speed things up, you slowed down. When we needed to slow things down, you were down the court with NO support. What were you thinking?! Are you TRYING to get me to bench you?" The point guard stared back at the coach without replying. His own fury was obvious; he was seething. The coach kept up his tirade. "What are YOU looking at?! You think it was a picnic watching you play? Go sit with him." He pointed with his thumb at the center on the end of the bench. "Maybe the two of you will remember how to play this game." As the point guard sidled toward the end of the bench, he was thinking how much he hated the coach and wondering how he might get back at him.

The coach was not done yet. He stared angrily at the remaining three of his starting team. "You three disgust me, too. If I had a dollar for every missed opportunity and every time you *let your man beat you to the ball, I could retire. What a sorry display of basketball! Go join them." He pointed to the previous two objects of his rage. "I want the five of you to come back and let me know your plan for improving your level of play. Until you do that, all five of you can just sit at the end of the bench. Now GO!" The three players walked to the end of the bench. Their emotional reactions were similar to those of the center and the point guard.*

What do you think the benched players are thinking and feeling? What do you think they are deciding? Do you think they have been motivated to play better? Would you want to play for this coach? What does this scenario have to do with parenting a child with special needs?

We have shared one of the worst examples of "time-out" out we could think of. (Yes, this is a fictional coach.) We're sure you will say, "I would never be that mean." We are equally sure that is true, and we hope this exaggerated example provides you with an opportunity to think about punitive time-out—even when it isn't as terrible as the scene just described.

A PROMISING IDEA UNFULFILLED

The concept of time-out was first introduced in the research literature by Charles Ferster in 1957; his original work was first with pigeons and then with chimpanzees. The exact phrase he used was "time-out from positive reinforcement."[4] Ferster's idea was that undesirable behavior could be reduced by removing his subjects and keeping them from experiencing the benefits of being with the group. Their desire to return to the group would motivate them to change their behavior. Within a few years, time-out began to be applied to children. Similarly, time away from their parents or their class was considered to be a motivating force for children to change their behavior and to increase their willingness to comply with adult expectations. An advantage of time-out was thought to be that it was considerably less punitive than more traditional forms of behavior management, like spanking.

It is sad that time-out, though perhaps less punitive than spanking, was designed as a punishment nonetheless. Children couldn't help but feel shamed when sent to time-out. With some alteration, the concept of time-out could have been in line with both Adlerian thinking and now-current brain research. It could have been a concept ahead of its time. The idea that when children were misbehaving a short break might enable them to self-soothe and even do some problem solving was a promising one indeed. Although it was certainly not articulated this way at the time, a time-out might have offered children the opportunity to get their "flipped lids" back in place (see page 35). From the perspective of what we now understand about how our brains work, time-out could have been a wonderful idea.

Unfortunately, the promise behind the idea was unrealized for almost thirty years, until it began to appear in Positive Discipline literature. Until then, time-out, as it was theorized and practiced, was not an opportunity to regain the ability to use the more rational, thinking parts of our brains; it was something more resembling a jail sentence. Kids were sent to time-out after committing infractions of one kind or another, and there even arose "sentencing guidelines." A still-popular notion holds that a child should go to time-out for one minute for each year of her age. Thus, a three-year-old, *any* three-year-old, is deemed to be able to sit in time-out for three minutes *and learn something from it!* Parents and teachers often add the ridiculous instruction to "think about what you did." This instruction is ridiculous because it assumes children will actually think about what they did. Instead, they are more likely to think about what the adult did and how to get even or avoid getting caught next time. Even sadder is the child who is thinking, "I'm a bad person," a developing belief that can affect the rest of his or her life. Punitive time-out certainly does not motivate improved behavior—except in

> Punitive time-out certainly does not motivate improved behavior— except in the child who is becoming an "approval junkie," based on a need to belong even at great cost to his or her sense of self-worth.

the child who is becoming an "approval junkie," based on a need to belong even at great cost to his or her sense of self-worth.

Not surprisingly from a Positive Discipline perspective, as soon as time-out began to be used, and seen by children, as a punishment, power struggles ensued. It is not at all uncommon to hear a parent tell a story about giving her child a time-out and the child refusing to go. What often follows is a protracted struggle about when and if the child will actually go to time-out. Frequently, the battle over children's willingness to go to time-out overshadows whatever misbehavior they first demonstrated.

Because time-out was not practiced as something helpful but used instead as a punishment, any usefulness it might have had disappeared. Roslyn Duffy, in a September 1996 article in *Child Care Information Exchange*,[5] describes a teacher responding to one child's hitting a playmate by giving the student a time-out. "Although the words 'AND SUFFER' remain unspoken, they reverberate in the air. Children hear the unspoken 'suffer' loud and clear." Like any other punishment, time-out was considered ineffective unless it hurt. The right number of minutes was calculated in a pseudo-scientific attempt to have the punishment hurt just enough but not too much.

A question we have asked ourselves many times in numerous Positive Discipline books and presentations is *Where did we get this crazy idea that in order to help children do better, we must first make them feel worse?* We believe that the reverse is true. *Children do better when they feel better.* This does not mean that we advocate not holding children accountable for their behavior. It does mean that, in teaching them to be accountable, we should treat them with dignity and respect and keep the long-term view in mind. We not only want the "misbehavior" to stop; we also want our children to develop life skills for good character.

As explained in chapter 3, children cannot learn in an atmosphere of fear and shame. Helping children *feel better* is another way of creating an atmosphere

> Where did we get this crazy idea that in order to help children do better, we must first make them feel worse? Children do better when they feel better.

of safety and encouragement so they can access the rational part of their brains and be open to learning.

Let's return to our example of the Tigers' time-out. Sometimes it is easier to see the effects of what we do to and with children when we reexamine the same situation, putting adults in the child's role. It is highly unlikely that a professional coach, or any good coach for that matter, would try to motivate players the way this fictional coach tried to. Yet many parents and teachers think that it is helpful to use punitive time-outs to get children to change their behavior; and some of those parents and teachers send children to time-out with the same kinds of blaming and shaming messages that the fictional coach used.

PUNITIVE VS. POSITIVE

What actually does happen when a sports team takes a time-out? Let's take a look.

> When the Tigers arrived at the bench, they all knew they weren't playing well. As they sat down, each looked at the floor. Their coach spoke. "Okay, we're down sixteen; tough game. Not our best one. Let's everyone breathe for a bit." He waved the ball boy over and asked him to fan the players with a towel, as it was very hot in the arena. The players sat and drank from their water bottles, feeling the slight but welcome breeze blow over them.
>
> The coach took up his portable whiteboard and started drawing Xs and Os on it. The players leaned in as the coach helped them devise a new strategy. He talked quickly about tightening up the defense so that the other team could not keep scoring. The point guard suggested that they put two players on the opposing point guard and try to force some errors the team could take advantage of. The coach also talked about what kind of shots they would need to make in order to claw their way back

to having a chance at winning the game. The center pointed out that no one would be expecting him to take three-point shots, as centers usually played closer to the basket and three-pointers were long-distance shots. The coach looked at him and nod-ded. "Good idea. Let's try and open it up for you to do that."

The horn sounded; the team's time-out was over. The play-ers and the coach stood in a circle. The coach put his hand in the middle of the circle, looked around, and said, "Team!" The players all extended their hands into the middle and echoed, "Team!"

What was different about the second scenario? To begin with, there was no blaming and shaming. The point of the time-out was not to make the players feel worse. It was to encourage them to feel better so that they might play better. They did some breathing. Two other things that helped them feel better were drinks of water and being fanned in order to cool off. Finally, they worked together to come up with a plan to play better. The whole process was about *encouragement*.

Contrast this approach with the kind of time-out children often are given. We require them to stand in corners or to sit in "naughty chairs." We might tell them to sit on their beds but *not* to play with toys or look at books. Instead, they should be thinking about what they have done. Access to books, toys, comfy blankets, or stuffed animals presumably might get in the way of this. Not surprisingly, children usually do not think about what they have done. Instead they fall prey to one of the Four *R*s of Punishment:

1. Resentment ("This is unfair; I can't trust adults.")

2. Revenge ("The adults are winning now, but I'll get even.")

3. Rebellion ("I'll do just the opposite to prove I don't have to do it their way.")

4. Retreat, in the form of sneakiness ("I won't get caught next time.") or reduced self-esteem ("I am a bad person.")

Punitive time-outs tend to be given in moments when everyone is angry, a time we know (from current brain research) is the least likely for effective problem solving to occur. Nevertheless, many parents and teachers try to deal with a child's behavior problem when they (the parents *and/or* the children) are in the flipped-lid state of brain functioning. An understanding of how our brains work tells us that this is useless. Children can't learn anything positive or helpful when they feel threatened. In those flipped-lid moments, they are capable only of fight, flight, or freeze. Their versions of these responses might be emotional withdrawal (flight), defying their parents in the moment or planning later revenge or rebellion (fight), or simply a blank stare (freeze). In those moments, lectures are useless at best because our children aren't capable of taking in that kind of information. At worst, lectures end up fueling resentment or a desire for revenge.

Let us repeat: Punitive time-out is not effective in the long run because children are not "thinking about what they did." They are thinking about how to get even, about how to avoid detection, or that they are "bad."

POSITIVE TIME-OUT

Positive time-out is based on an understanding of the brain and of human nature, i.e., that children (and adults) do better when they feel better. Take a moment to ponder that thought, because it is very important. If you truly believed that you could help your child do better by helping him or her feel better, what would time-out look like? Chances are it would be a pleasant place designed by children, or at least with their input, to help them soothe themselves and calm down. It might also involve a parent or a teacher going to this place with them to help them feel better until they can regain access to the rational, thinking parts of their brains. A common objection (by adults, not by children) to positive time-out is the fear that it is "rewarding the misbehavior" and that children will use it to *avoid* dealing with things that might be uncomfortable for them. In fact, children are usually far more willing to *engage* in problem solving when they are calm.

In order for a positive time-out space to fulfill its role as a place for children to feel better, it is a good idea to ask the children to give it a different name. As much as we would like it to be different, the term *time-out* does not evoke encouraging images of a sports team taking a break to rest, regather, and plan. For most of our children, *time-out* is a loaded term; it evokes very negative feelings. A social worker in Portland, Oregon, tells the story of when he first went to work at a residential treatment center for children. He was chatting with a group of boys, and they were all excitedly trying to talk at the same time. Laughing, the social worker made his hands into a T and said, "Whoa, slow down. Time out." All of the boys looked panicked; one of them asked, crying, "What did we do?"

We have found children, even as young as preschool age, to be very creative in giving their positive time-out space a name. One class decided to call their positive time-out area "Space." The teacher brought dark blue netting and hung it from the ceiling in a corner. The children colored planets and stars that were hung from the ceiling. In another class, the children decorated a giant cardboard box, decided (in class meetings) to put books, pillows, blankets, and stuffed animals in it, and called it "the Cave." In a preschool class, the children called their space "Alaska," and their creative teacher quickly added the subtitle "A Place to Cool Off."

Parents can help their children create, name, and stock positive time-out spaces in their homes as well. While it certainly is nice if a family lives in a home big enough to accommodate a separate area for a positive time-out space, it is decidedly not a requirement. Families who live in small apartments have creative children who can be part of a process to designate a space as well. One young child of our acquaintance told his father that he wanted his "feel-better place" to be under his bed. He was very comforted by the tight fit under the bed and kept some very special toys and stuffed animals there to help him feel better. (It is unclear whether the dust bunnies were a comfort or not.)

An important aspect of positive time-out is to allow children to "choose" it. In this way the old "You go take a time-out!" is replaced by "Would it help you to go to the Cave?" Of course, when a child is in a flipped-lid state, she might be too irrational to choose anything. It is then helpful to ask, "Would you like me to go with you?" Some children find this offer comforting enough that it helps them start the process of calming. Others will decline or, more likely, keep on tantrumming. If the child is not in any physical danger and is not threatening to throw or break things, a teacher or parent can say something like, "Okay, I'm going to the Cave to feel better. Come join me if you feel like it." Watching you go might serve as enough of a surprise to the child's limbic system that the prefrontal cortex and mirror neurons are able to kick in and start the soothing process and inspire her to follow you. Other children simply may need time to "feel their feelings" without being rescued or "fixed." Standing nearby and offering "energetic support" (see chapter 12) may be the kind of positive time-out that some children need.

In a preschool classroom, Joel, an early childhood specialist you will meet in chapter 7, was very frustrated as he tried to have a class meeting with his group of children. Almost no one was cooperating, and Joel found himself on the verge of shouting. Instead, he got up and announced, "I am too frustrated to finish our meeting now. I'm going to the Cave until I feel a little better." The group fell silent and watched with their mouths open as he wedged himself into the Cave. "Are you mad at us?" one child asked. "Nope," said Joel. "I was so frustrated that our meeting was too loud, and I needed to take a break." Another child asked, "Are you coming back?" Joel replied, "You know, I am feeling much better. I think I will come back now." It would be nice to report that the rest of the class meeting proceeded smoothly. The truth was that it was just as chaotic, but a couple of very important things happened. First, in a calmer state, Joel really was able to handle the chaos more helpfully. Second, Joel's actions provided the children with a wonderful model of an adult using positive time-out to feel better.

If a child's tantrum presents a danger to either himself or others or he is throwing and breaking things, it may be necessary to *bring* him to the positive time-out space. While bringing the child there, the parent or teacher should make every effort to remain calm, patient, and kind. It can help to *move slowly* with the child so that he doesn't feel rushed and further provoked. It is also vital in those situations that the adult stay there with him to provide emotional support. When a child's flipped-lid state makes him so inaccessible, it is all the more reason that he needs a calm adult to demonstrate caring and concern.

A valid concern that can be raised at this point is whether the very act of *bringing* a child to the positive time-out space can turn into, or exacerbate, a power struggle. This may be especially true for a child whose mistaken goal at that moment is either misguided power or revenge. Unfortunately, there are no foolproof guidelines for making this decision. If a child's safety (or someone else's) is clearly at risk, physically moving her may, in fact, be the best option. In our experience, what has fueled the power struggles that have ensued from these decisions has been the adult's rapid movements, uncomfortable and restrictive hold of the child, unpleasant tone of voice, and, ultimately, need to "win" the struggle. To the extent that parents and teachers are able to remain calm and supportive during the move, this can act as a damper on the child's rage.

In addition, it is important to remember that positive time-out isn't the only tool in your toolbox. It could be more appropriate to calmly sit by a child offering *energetic support* until his temper cools. Some children are distracted from a tantrum when they hear a request for a hug, a request for help, or validation of their feelings or when they are shown the Anger Wheel of Choice (more on the Anger Wheel of Choice in chapter 7).

A STATE OF MIND AS MUCH AS A PLACE

As we noted above, for some children with many of the conditions that can be considered "special needs," moving from one spot to another, especially in a flipped-lid moment, can be a very difficult undertaking. An important aspect of positive time-out to keep in mind is that it should be *helpful*. If moving your child with special needs is more traumatic than comforting, it is wise to consider how to bring positive time-out to her. When doing this, it may also be necessary to clear the on-the-spot time-out space of people and objects/furniture to reduce the risk of anyone getting hurt.

Lisa, the parent of Violet, a little girl with autism spectrum disorder, described how she tried and failed repeatedly to help her seven-year-old daughter use positive time-out to feel better. Once Violet was out of sorts, Lisa reported, she could neither hear her mother's suggestion to go to their "feel-better" place nor tolerate being taken there. When Lisa tried to go herself (to model cooling off), her daughter would become self-hurtful and start banging her head. The strategy that this mother came up with was to bring the beanbag from their feel-better place to her daughter. At first, Violet just lay down on the beanbag, clearly comforted. Over the course of only a few days, she was able to nod "yes" when Lisa asked her if her beanbag would help her feel better. They are now working on trying to help Violet go to the feel-better place on her own when she is so upset. With Violet seeming to understand the value of calming down, Lisa is optimistic that this is a skill she can learn.

SOME COMMUNICATION ADAPTATIONS RELATED TO POSITIVE TIME-OUT

Children in the flipped-lid state may be more receptive to positive time-out if you present information in the form of visual representations in addition to words. For example, you can express empathy by showing feeling pictures. You can remind your children of the special place by showing a photograph of it, and you can display, in the positive time-out area, a picture of a child in a relaxed, calm state. With a two-sided board, you can show the picture of the positive time-out area on one side. On the other side, you can show the child the activity that will happen once he feels better. Below are some communication adaptations that can help transform your child's upsetting experience into a positive one:

- Feeling pictures (six common ones are happy, sad, angry, scared, frustrated, and disappointed)

- A photograph of the positive time-out space

- A photograph or a line drawing representing *relaxed* or *calm*

- A two-sided board with a photo of the positive time-out space on one side and Velcro on the reverse side (to which any useful picture can be attached)

Steven, a coauthor of this book, shares an example of using the Positive Discipline tool of asking for a hug in conjunction with positive time-out. The child in the story was in a social-skills class and had both severe articulation problems and delays in other areas of his development.

Today a four-year-old boy stormed away from the art table, screaming that he was "mad, frustrated, and not happy." My assistant followed him over to our comfy cushion (our positive time-out area) where he had wrapped himself in a blanket, now just screaming wordlessly and kicking the cushion. He refused to talk to the assistant and just continued to scream. I sat next to him and whispered, "I need a hug." He continued screaming and writhing. After about fifteen seconds, I repeated, "I need a hug." He stopped screaming and flailing but kept his back to me. Ten more seconds. "I need a hug." After a long pause, he turned over, climbed into my lap, and hugged me. I asked him if he wanted to go back to the art table by himself or if he wanted me to go with him. He asked me to go with him. He went back, finished his project happily, and left the table.

Of course, positive time-out is just one of the many Positive Discipline tools that will be discussed in the upcoming chapters of this book. It is important to remember that no one tool is effective for every child in every situation. The emphasis throughout this book is on determining which Positive Discipline tools will be most effective in a given situation for a child, and, if necessary, adapting them to make them more accessible for children with special needs.

5

HANNAH'S STORY: ACKNOWLEDGE AND SUPPORT YOUR WHOLE CHILD

As a four-year-old with autism, Hannah had a limited ability to speak. However, her skills at sustaining her attention to the details of pictures in books, figuring out how to accomplish complicated motor tasks, and using her imagination with small toy characters led her parents and teachers to suspect that she was "high functioning." While Hannah's mother routinely brought her to a three-times-a-week play group, Hannah arrived one day with an aunt who was taking care of her while both parents were on a business trip for a week. On that day, the first morning routines at school were going well for Hannah. She played independently with a variety of toys during choice time, and she sat in circle time, showing her usual high level of interest in the visual displays that the teacher used in the activities. After circle time, when it was time to gather with her classmates at the doorway before going to the gym, her teacher gave her a picture of the gym from a visual schedule display and told Hannah, "It's time to go to the gym."

Usually, Hannah took the picture, examined it, and then started walking to the gym, but today she responded quite differently. She threw the picture, began to cry, and then fell to the floor. Hannah seemed very sad and was unable to be consoled by her teacher's soft voice and offers of a comforting hug. It did not help when the teacher tried to point out that the other kids were waiting at the doorway or that many of Hannah's favorite toys were available in the gym. Her teacher suspected that Hannah was upset not only because there had been a change in her usual routine this morning, given the absence of her mother, but because she truly missed her mother and had no way of explaining her sense of loss.

With this in mind, her teacher gathered paper and markers and began to draw the story of Hannah's dilemma while saying, "Hannah is sad," "Mommy and Daddy are not at home," "Mommy and Daddy drove to a hotel," "Mommy and Daddy will come home in five days," "Hannah will be happy," "Mommy and Daddy will be happy." Hannah stopped crying when her teacher mentioned "Mommy," and she watched intently as her teacher drew simple pictures while telling the story. When her teacher paused between drawings, Hannah pushed her teacher's hand to draw more. On a number of occasions in the next two class sessions, Hannah found paper and markers in the classroom and brought these to her teacher to have the story and drawings repeated. In addition to reviewing with Hannah the story about her emotions, her teacher acknowledged Hannah's every attempt to respond to requests. The outcome during that week was very positive: The unhappy expressions of emotion that Hannah had displayed earlier in the week when transitioning did not happen again.

Hannah's teacher was successful in helping Hannah calm down because she considered not only the behavior that Hannah displayed and what seemed to be a trigger (a request to transition) but also Hannah's life as a whole. A traditional special education perspective might have led the teacher to notice only what was externally observed: the request to transition and Hannah's refusal to go to the gym with the rest of the class. Instead, the teacher considered Hannah's feelings about the absence of her parents as well as the changes that Hannah experienced in her daily routines while being cared for by her aunt. Her teacher's awareness of Hannah's interest in and ability to comprehend pictures, combined with Hannah's significant limitation in talking about thoughts and feelings, led this teacher to consider an alternative method to communicate empathy and understanding. Based on her knowledge of "the whole child," Hannah's teacher could respond with greater thoughtfulness and effectiveness.

Your success with your child with special needs will be greatly enhanced when you see and relate to your child as a whole. When your child is challenged, her whole being is challenged: thoughts, feelings, and behaviors combined. She is not simply "a child with challenging behaviors." To help your child, try to understand what she is experiencing in her life, within her family, and with others outside the family. Consider how her disability impacts her experience of life's challenges. The more you are able to understand what makes your child unique as a whole person, the better able you will be to select tools for support and guidance that will lead to her development of long-term socially useful skills.

> Your success with your child with special needs will be greatly enhanced when you see and relate to your child as a whole. When your child is challenged, her whole being is challenged: thoughts, feelings, and behaviors combined.

> The more you are able to understand what makes your child unique as a whole person, the better able you will be to select tools for support and guidance that will lead to her development of long-term socially useful skills.

THE POSITIVE DISCIPLINE TOOLS RELATED TO YOUR WHOLE CHILD

In order to acknowledge and support your whole child, we suggest that you create opportunities for your child to develop affirmative self-beliefs. As a practitioner of Positive Discipline, you will help your child develop these two important beliefs:

- I have the ability to understand my feelings and can exhibit self-control.
- I can respond to the experiences of everyday life with responsibility, adaptability, flexibility, and integrity.

Hannah's teacher responded to Hannah's upset by supporting her and helping her develop positive beliefs about herself. She drew and talked about Hannah's feelings instead of ignoring them and simply trying to stop the behaviors. She provided her with an alternative way to process her feelings, via listening to and looking at a story, which ultimately enabled Hannah to demonstrate *self-control*. In response to her teacher's efforts, Hannah took *responsibility* for maintaining and initiating conversations about her situation. She demonstrated *adaptability* to the situation given the empathic provision of information by the teacher. She showed *flexibility* in her thinking because the visuals helped her view her circumstances differently. And she demonstrated *integrity* by engaging with her teacher in a mutually respectful manner.

THE POSITIVE DISCIPLINE TOOLS RELATED TO YOUR CHILD'S MISTAKEN GOAL

While it is important to use Positive Discipline tools to support your whole child, it will also be helpful to understand the belief behind her behaviors and the corresponding mistaken goal. This will allow you to use

Positive Discipline's proactive and encouraging responses to help your child experience belonging and significance in socially useful ways. In the scenario with Hannah, Hannah's teacher felt ineffectual when Hannah didn't transition in her usual smooth fashion and didn't respond to comforting. The teacher's feelings of inadequacy (her first clue that Hannah's mistaken goal was assumed inadequacy) continued as Hannah remained unresponsive to efforts to redirect her attention to other children or to remind her of favorite toys in the gym. Her teacher resisted the urge to react by giving up (walking away) or by overhelping Hannah (walking her through the transition). Instead, she took note of the actions that Hannah had decided to engage in and "read" the coded message underlying her actions: "Don't give up on me. Show me a small step."

If your child is acting out of the mistaken goal of assumed inadequacy, you can use Positive Discipline's proactive and encouraging responses related to this mistaken goal. These responses are highlighted in the following pages, with Hannah's story as an example of how to apply them.

Break Tasks Down into Small Steps

In the scenario about Hannah, her teacher used a story drawing to help Hannah understand the sequence of her parents' travels. The initial step in the process for Hannah was to see and listen to the story. Her teacher did not initially require Hannah to stand up or move in the direction of the classroom door. You can help your child by viewing the overall skill/expectation as a sequence of small steps and teaching your child to carry out just one small step at a time.

Stop All Criticism

Throughout her interactions with Hannah, the teacher remained calm, kind, and caring. She did not reprimand Hannah when she didn't follow the request to transition to the doorway with her classmates. Your composed, benign response to your child when she engages in undesired behavior will help you to not disparage your child for the misguided behavior but instead to support your child's ability to behave more favorably.

Encourage Any Positive Attempt

Hannah's teacher focused on understanding and communicating about Hannah's feelings and the suspected reasons for her sadness. She did not focus on Hannah's behavior of falling to the floor and discontinuing the transition to the doorway. Also, the teacher responded to Hannah's nonverbally communicated request to have the story retold, and she recognized Hannah whenever she cooperated with requests. When you respond favorably to any attempt on the part of your child to carry out part or all of the expected behavior, you are providing information to your child that can lead her to understand that the task is attainable.

Have Faith in Your Child's Abilities

When Hannah's teacher saw how favorably Hannah responded to the story about feelings and her parents' trip, she felt more confident that Hannah could recover from her upset. As you consider any necessary modifications in the expected task related to your child's special need and you present an expectation small enough for your child to accomplish, you can trust that she will have the ability to be successful.

Focus on Assets

Hannah's teacher capitalized on Hannah's strengths: her attentiveness to the details of visual information and her basic understanding of sequence. Hannah's teacher "listened" to Hannah's nonverbal message to repeat the story. You can effectively make use of your child's strengths and incorporate these to help your child accomplish a difficult task.

Don't Engage in Pity

Hannah's teacher *empathized* with her. Empathy is very different from pity. She communicated through drawings that she understood Hannah's feelings. She was not embarrassed or disappointed that Hannah was so overcome by emotion. Your child will be helped when you and others attempt to understand your child's feelings about a situation, not when you feel pity for the child because of the misguided behavior.

Don't Give Up

Hannah's teacher persisted in searching for positive solutions that would help Hannah to self-manage. She did not physically walk Hannah through the requested transition. She waited for Hannah to take the initiative. Your child with special needs will continue to learn new skills. During this process, you will have the opportunity to practice patience while your child's process of gaining new social skills takes time to develop.

Set Up Opportunities for Success

Hannah's teacher remained within close proximity of Hannah, communicating through her body language that she was available to her. Positioned close to Hannah in this way, she could be attentive and encourage any attempts by Hannah to independently walk to the door. Consider how you might orchestrate the situation so that your child experiences success, even for slight attempts to meet the expectation.

Teach Skills

Hannah's teacher taught her to respond to and communicate through pictures as a way of processing Hannah's more abstract experiences of emotions. She acknowledged her whenever she followed a direction. Make the teaching of self-management and social skills a priority. The more your child acquires competence in these areas, the better he or she will be at responding favorably in challenging situations.

Show How but Don't Do For

Hannah's teacher refrained from physically moving Hannah through the expected response of walking to the doorway. Had she done this, there would have been increased risk of eliciting further upset in Hannah, who might have become unhappy about being forced to do something she wasn't ready to do. Instead, her teacher patiently waited for Hannah to regain control and walk on her own.

In a similar situation with your own child, try modeling the desired behavior for her, and practice waiting patiently for her to imitate the preferred action independently. If your child is not yet skilled at imitating, gently help her to perform the action. Provide this type of support initially if you feel no physical resistance from your child. As you "show how" in this fashion, "listen with your hands," that is, when you literally *feel* any physical movement from your child to independently complete part or all of the action, gradually remove your support. We understand that there are times when waiting patiently will be difficult. Think of waiting patiently as a goal to strive for. The striving is good; accepting that we will sometimes come up short is critical.

Build on Interests

Knowing that Hannah liked to look at the details of pictures, the teacher used drawings to communicate empathy and understanding to Hannah. Hannah's interest in her parents made the content of the teacher's stories motivating for Hannah to focus on. Use your child's interests to get and maintain attention on the skill you are teaching.

Encourage

Hannah's teacher gave statements of encouragement whenever Hannah followed through on requests, for example, "Thank you, Hannah, for putting your lunch box away." The words you use to encourage your child, phrased not as praise but as statements about your child's positive actions, will help your child to learn about socially useful behavior.

Use Class/Family Meetings

If Hannah's lack of cooperation with her teacher's requests had continued, the teacher might have addressed the topic during the daily circle time activity. For example, with Hannah and her preschool-aged classmates in the play group, the teacher might have brainstormed with the group what to do when they felt very sad. Drawing pictures to "list" the brainstormed suggestions could have helped the children to understand the ideas shared. Also, the teacher might have used a role-play activity for the children to practice how to recover from upsets. In the context of a role play during the class meeting, Hannah and her classmates could have observed and considered solutions to their challenges. Your family/class meetings can be invaluable for addressing concerns outside the context of the situations that lead you to be concerned. Your child's input at the meeting can help him or her to see a variety of options for responding to challenges. Consider your child's developmental ability and special needs as you choose the type of visual mode to document ideas at the meeting (drawings, printed words, et cetera.)

Enjoy Your Child

Hannah's teacher truly enjoyed Hannah. She came to view the challenges that Hannah experienced as opportunities to discover positive ways to help Hannah learn social skills that would enable her to be successful throughout her life. Find ways to enjoy your child. This journey that you're on with your child can be a chance to make new discoveries that lead you both to a stronger, more connected relationship.

REVIEW OF POSITIVE DISCIPLINE TOOLS PRESENTED IN THIS CHAPTER

1. Help your child to develop the belief *I have the ability to understand my feelings and can exhibit self-control.*
2. Help your child develop the belief *I can respond to the experiences of everyday life with responsibility, adaptability, flexibility, and integrity.*
3. Break tasks down into small steps.
4. Stop all criticism.
5. Encourage any positive attempt.
6. Have faith in your child's abilities.
7. Focus on assets.
8. Don't engage in pity.
9. Don't give up.
10. Set up opportunities for success.

11. Teach skills.
12. Show how but don't do for.
13. Build on interests.
14. Encourage.
15. Use class/family meetings.
16. Enjoy your child.

JAMIE'S STORY: STRENGTHEN YOUR CHILD'S SENSE OF BELONGING AND SIGNIFICANCE

Three-year-old Jamie loved to play with toy cars and trucks. Before he was a year old, he enjoyed lying with his head on the floor watching the wheels of his little toy vehicles as he rolled them back and forth. When he was diagnosed with autism spectrum disorder at the age of eighteen months, one of the evaluators recommended to his parents that they limit his time playing with toy vehicles. She believed that this repetitive behavior was likely reducing his time learning about and playing with other toys, and because he preferred to play in a solitary fashion with his little vehicles, it was interfering with his ability to learn how to play with others.

Jamie's parents took to heart every suggestion that was given to them about their son. When they returned home, they packed up all the toy vehicles into a large box and stored the box on a shelf in a closet. They decided that they would bring out only a few of them at a time, and for limited amounts of time each day. Apparently, not all the vehicles were packed away, because as his parents were discussing their strategy, Jamie entered the room, with a smile on his face, holding a little car. Jamie's father, Jack, quickly took the toy car out of his hand and said, "Let's go find your puzzles." Jamie looked shocked, and then his face contorted with upset. "Car? Car?" he said, with desperation in his voice. Jack responded, "Let's go play with puzzles, Jamie." When Jamie persisted, "Car? Car?" Jack walked out of the room. Instead of following his father, Jamie fell to the floor and screamed, "Car!" in a very unhappy tone of voice. While twisting his body and rolling back and forth on the floor, he began to scream and cry mournfully. Jack remained in the other room, trying to decide if he was doing the right thing while he waited for Jamie to calm down and join him in puzzle play.

All children, including children with special needs, strive to experience belonging and significance in their families and communities. Jamie initially exhibited behaviors that suggest that he did, indeed, feel a sense of belonging and significance. He entered the room with his parents. He demonstrated that he felt safe and a sense of connection (belonging) in their presence by smiling as he held his little car.

> All children, including children with special needs, strive to experience belonging and significance in their families and communities.

When Jack grabbed the car without asking permission to take it, Jamie's emotional reaction was one of surprise. He eventually displayed signs of frustration and distress because his subsequent series of communications ("Car? Car?") was ignored. Jamie's emotional responses were legitimate and appropriate reactions to his experiences. He continued to communicate to his father, albeit with distress in his voice, suggesting that Jamie believed he could still connect (belong) and that his message was important enough to be heard (significant). Eventually, it appeared that Jamie's sense of belonging and significance began to erode when Jack (from Jamie's perspective) ignored his distress and failed to acknowledge what Jamie was communicating to him. Jamie's fall to the floor likely reflected his growing despair at the sudden and unexplained loss of his car and his frustration about not getting his message across. His further escalation of discouraged behavior (screaming, crying, and rolling on the floor) probably was a signal that at that moment Jamie did not feel as though he either belonged or was significant.

When your child with special needs behaves in ways that are not socially useful, making use of Positive Discipline tools will affirm his sense of belonging and significance as you help him learn alternative ways to behave. Because your child's ability to understand the meaning of words or interactions may be compromised by the nature of his handicapping condition, you may need to adjust your communication and actions so that your message, confirming and supporting your child's sense of belonging and significance, is clearly received.

> Because your child's ability to understand the meaning of words or interactions may be compromised by the nature of his handicapping condition, you may need to adjust your communication and actions so that your message, confirming and supporting your child's sense of belonging and significance, is clearly received.

POSITIVE DISCIPLINE TOOLS FOR STRENGTHENING YOUR CHILD'S SENSE OF BELONGING AND SIGNIFICANCE

Let's replay the above scenario with Jamie, and this time imagine that Jamie's father had used Positive Discipline tools in this situation. While Jamie's father might still have been concerned that Jamie had found the vehicle, he would have approached Jamie with greater warmth and understanding. (He might also have realized that having the car was *not a problem from Jamie's perspective*.) Instead of taking the car from Jamie,

Jack might have commented about the toy and, more important, Jamie's apparent feeling about it: "You found a car! You are happy about the car!" Jack might then have encouraged some expanded play ideas related to the car: "What can you do with your car?" Further, Jack might have taken this opportunity to teach social skills by asking for a turn to hold and play with the car so he could model the expanded play ideas. Jack might have encouraged repeated opportunities for reciprocal turn taking, using words that Jamie might also be able to use in other situations: "your turn" (or "Jamie's turn") and "my turn" (or "Dad's turn").

Jack might have introduced puzzles more gradually, with an effort to help Jamie to easily and pleasantly shift his attention and interest from cars to puzzles. When it was Jack's turn to hold and play with the car, Jack might have driven it into the other room looking for an imaginary toy store. Jamie would likely have followed because he wanted the car, arriving in the other room without a struggle. Once there, Jack could have returned the car to Jamie, encouraging him to drive around the toy store. When it was Jack's turn again with the car, Jack could have driven to the puzzle shelves and pulled out a puzzle. Knowing about Jamie's interest in vehicles, Jack might have strategically pulled out a puzzle with this theme. With Jamie nearby, keeping a close watch on the car that Jack was holding, Jack might have playfully hidden the car under the puzzle (for Jamie to find) or pulled out a piece of the puzzle (enticing Jamie to complete it). The scenario might have continued like this, with Jack, at each of his turns with the car, presenting an extremely small challenge to Jamie with the intention of helping Jamie expand his play with a variety of toys. It is certainly possible that Jamie might not have been ready for these additional challenges and might simply have wanted his car back to play with in his own way. However, even if Jack had only helped Jamie to take turns (although orchestrated by Jack) and to move with ease to a different room with his car, these would have been significant accomplishments for Jamie.

If Jamie had grown stressed at any point when his father was holding the car, Jack could have reflected Jamie's feelings and voiced his son's message: "You sound worried. You want your car now!" By doing this, Jack would have acknowledged not only that he understood Jamie's communication but also that Jamie's message was important. In addition, Jack would have demonstrated empathy to Jamie, helping his son feel understood. And he would have provided Jamie with a label for this feeling, beginning the important job of building an emotional vocabulary and, as Stanley Greenspan put it, "emotional thinking."[6]

In this revised scenario, Jamie's father strengthened his son's sense of belonging and significance by applying seven very important Positive Discipline tools:

- Make sure the message of love gets through.
- Provide connection before correction.
- Listen to "get into the child's world."
- Reflect and/or validate feelings.
- Take time for training.
- Be kind and firm at the same time.
- Use the three Rs of recovery.

In the revised scenario, Jamie's father demonstrated warmth and acceptance even though he was initially uncomfortable with Jamie's play with the car (*made sure the message of love got through*). He *listened* to Jamie and acknowledged his interest in the car (*connection before correction*) and then *took time for training* by engaging him in simple reciprocal turn taking using his object of interest. When Jamie became upset, Jack *reflected and validated his feelings*. Jack was *kind and firm* at the same time: kind to be respectful to Jamie and firm to meet the needs of the situation (helping Jamie learn new skills). All of these tools help Jamie develop a sense of belonging and significance while guiding him to learn the skills that are important to his growth and development.

Unfortunately, real life doesn't allow us to replay a scene with our child after we have inadvertently (but with the best of intentions) blown it. In the unrevised scenario, Jamie's father can recover from his mistake and attempt to restore emotional equilibrium for his son by using the Three *R*s of Recovery: Recognize, Reconcile, and Resolve. As we discussed in chapter 3, unintended mistakes in our interactions with our children are inevitable. If you make a mistake with your child, we encourage you to restore the connection between you and him and confirm that he is truly significant.

To bring your relationship with your child back into equilibrium, follow the Three *R*s of Recovery by *recognizing* your part in the mistake, *reconciling* with your child by communicating that you are sincerely sorry for how you handled the situation, and *resolving* it by engaging your child in problem solving. You have probably experienced how forgiving children are when you apologize. This simple act creates a connection before you go on to the correction phase of working on a solution together.

> To bring your relationship with your child back into equilibrium, follow the Three *R*s of Recovery by *recognizing* your part in the mistake, *reconciling* with your child by communicating that you are sincerely sorry for how you handled the situation, and *resolving* it by engaging your child in problem solving.

If your child has limited receptive language and doesn't understand the abstract concepts associated with the Three *R*s of Recovery, you might (1) use simple language to admit that you made a mistake (e.g., "Uh-oh! Daddy made a mistake!"), (2) show empathy for your child's upset that was elicited by your actions (e.g., "You are sad," combined with a sad facial expression and sad tone of voice), and (3) in simple terms, seek a solution (e.g., "Would it help if Daddy gave back the car?").

Making sure the message of love gets through, providing connection before correction, and practicing the Three *R*s of Recovery (when appropriate) will greatly fortify your child's sense of belonging and significance. In addition to these Positive Discipline tools and the others mentioned above, your understanding of the mistaken belief behind your child's behavior and his corresponding mistaken goal will once again shed light on the kinds of proactive and encouraging responses that will strengthen your child's sense of belonging and significance.

THE POSITIVE DISCIPLINE TOOLS RELATED
TO YOUR CHILD'S MISTAKEN GOAL

It took less than three minutes for Jamie to shift from a happy boy holding his beloved car to a highly distressed and disengaged child. Yet the underlying beliefs that led to Jamie's decisions about how to react, combined with the beliefs that guided Jack's decisions about how to respond, are complex. An examination of the interactions between Jamie and his dad through the lens of the Mistaken Goal Chart (see chapter 2) gives clues about Jamie's mistaken goal as well as about encouraging ways that his dad might respond.

Jamie's intense focus on toy cars was *innocent*. A behavior like this, which involves a significant preoccupation with certain things or ideas that is unusual in emphasis or degree, is one of the characteristics of autism spectrum disorder. Jack *mistakenly interpreted* this behavior as a challenge, as if Jamie had directed the behavior at him. Jack's response, snatching the car from Jamie's hands without asking permission, arose from his own belief that Jamie needed to expand his repertoire of play and Jack's subsequent determination to *make* Jamie stop focusing on cars. In response to his father's actions, Jamie did not follow his father into the room with the puzzles and instead intensified his focus on the car (fell on the floor and screamed, "Car!"). Jamie's behavior further escalated to rolling on the floor while screaming and crying.

Jamie's increased upset about losing his car, clearly reflected in his subsequent behaviors, was significantly provoked by Jack's actions. These actions, in turn, resulted from Jack's feelings of being threatened and challenged by Jamie's initial innocent behavior. Jamie's escalation may have been further affected by his legitimate desire for his father's attention to and acknowledgment of his communication. Jack had ignored Jamie's innocent request for the car (due to Jack's mistaken interpretation), which led Jamie to behave in ways that were, indeed, socially directed; at that point

> A child's innocent behavior can be transformed into mistaken-goal behavior as a result of the adult's response to the innocent behavior.

Jamie really *was* directing his behavior *at* Jack. This is a clear example of how a child's innocent behavior can be transformed into mistaken-goal behavior as a result of the adult's response to the innocent behavior.

Given Jack's feelings (threatened and challenged) and actions (taking the car and walking away), the mistaken goal related to Jamie's socially directed actions was misguided power. The mistaken belief behind Jamie's behaviors was "I belong and am significant only if I am in control and when no one bosses me." The coded message related to this mistaken goal is "Let me help. Give me choices."

If your child is acting out of the mistaken goal of misguided power, Positive Discipline offers many valuable and useful tools. In addition to the tools mentioned above, we will discuss the following eight Positive Discipline tools that could have been helpful in Jamie's scenario. Some are tools that were mentioned above; in addition, the importance of the tool of being kind and firm at the same time is discussed in greater detail.

- Redirect your child to positive power by asking for help.
- Offer limited choices.
- Be firm and kind at the same time.
- Decide what you will do.
- Let routines be the boss.
- Use the four steps for winning cooperation.
- Remember that your child will listen to you after he feels listened to.
- Use family/class meetings.

It is so important to know that there is never just one way to handle a challenging behavior.

It is so important to know that there is never just one way to handle a challenging behavior. You will feel more encouraged when you have several possibilities so you can choose what seems most appropriate at the time.

Redirect Your Child to Positive Power by Asking for Help

It's not very likely that a child who is *helping* a parent or teacher will simultaneously be struggling with that adult. The very act of helping can lead a child to feel a personal, constructive power related to what he can accomplish and to feel control over some part of his environment. Given the diminished sense of personal power and control that a child with special needs can often experience due to the limitations associated with his condition, requesting help from this child is very encouraging and validating. In the scenario with Jamie, his help might have been solicited from the outset. Jamie could have been asked to help put the car in a special place or to go help look for puzzles. If Jamie didn't understand the words alone, the information related to helping could have been presented more concretely: A special "clean-up" box routinely used for storing special toys could have been shown as he was being requested to help clean up. Or Jamie's dad might have himself retrieved a puzzle from the other room, begun assembling it near Jamie, and then asked Jamie to help him finish it.

Offer Limited Choices

Providing a child with choices will usually lead the child to an increased sense of control because ultimately the child (and not the adult) gets to choose. If Jack had given Jamie more choices in his play experiences, Jamie would have been less likely to feel that he was being controlled by his father. "Would you like to have your car 'watch' while we work on a puzzle or put it in your pocket while we work on a puzzle?" Sensing his own personal power, because he has choices, could lead a child like Jamie to experience power, not in a misguided way but in a developmentally appropriate and socially useful way.

In addition, as a way of redirecting Jamie's attention to other toys, Jack might have provided Jamie with other attractive play options, such as jumping on a mini trampoline or looking at a favorite book. When a child on the autism spectrum, like Jamie, is so focused on a favorite toy, it can be very difficult for him to even consider playing with another one.

Effortlessly shifting focus of attention is a skill that he simply may not have yet acquired. By bringing a few choices to Jamie, Jack might have helped his son in the short run to shift attention to other possibilities and in the long run to make shifting activities that much easier.

Be Firm and Kind at the Same Time

Jack's removal of the car from Jamie's hand was firm but certainly not kind. In fact, it reflected a negative quality of firmness: insensitivity to Jamie's feelings. To demonstrate kindness and firmness at the same time, Jack would have needed to demonstrate warmth and understanding to Jamie while also employing respectful ways to limit Jamie's time with the car in order to expand his play. Further, Jack maintained his firm disposition with Jamie when he ignored Jamie's pleas for the car and when he walked out of the room. Again, both of these actions illustrated a negative aspect of firmness: lack of acknowledgment of the child's message and, more acutely, of the child's very presence. When your child with special needs is beginning to engage in actions that suggest that more problematic behaviors will follow, that's a critical time when your kind availability and firm guidance is needed. Being fully present to your child at these times, in a gentle and calming way, can help to circumvent a struggle, or at least to lessen the intensity if one should occur.

Decide What You Will Do

Deciding what you will do, instead of what you will make your child do, is a respectful way to avoid power struggles. In Jamie's case, his father might have brought some puzzles into the same room where Jamie was holding his car. Jack himself might have begun playing with a puzzle, or with any other toy that might be of interest to Jamie besides cars. Having these other toys present and seeing his father playing with them might have enticed Jamie to try one of those toys himself. Deciding what you will do leaves open the possibility that your child will make a favorable decision about what he will do. If the decision comes from your child and not from you, conflicts will more likely be avoided.

Let Routines Be the Boss

Giving up preferred toys or stopping favorite activities is an unpleasant experience for many children. This experience can be more intensified for children on the autism spectrum because they may not understand the reason for stopping the activity or for giving up the toy. To assist your child in ending play with a toy or a preferred activity, use a routine to be the "boss." This has the added benefit of taking a parent or a teacher out of the role of "authority figure." You can simply remind your child of the routine (e.g., clean up toys before bath time; end the video before dinner) and try to remain emotionally neutral as you convey this message.

In Jack's attempt to keep Jamie from spending too much time playing with cars, he could have begun building a routine with Jamie: play with the car for a certain amount of time followed by play with another toy for a certain amount of time. The use of a timer could have been another "authority" that was built into the routine, so that Jack didn't have to be the "boss" who signaled to Jamie when to stop playing with the car. For many children who are on the autism spectrum (as well as for many who are not) it is helpful to have the routine posted in pictures. Line drawings or photographs provide visual information that is very helpful to children. For children with special needs who don't yet understand the meaning of pictures or who have a visual impairment, meaningful objects can be sequenced on a board to represent the routine. For example, a tiny car can represent play with cars, a bubble wand can represent the blowing bubbles activity, and a puzzle piece can represent play with puzzles. Knowing what to anticipate, through visual or concrete representations, assists children in making transitions with greater ease.

Use the Four Steps for Winning Cooperation

The four steps for winning cooperation are as follows:

1. Express understanding of the child's feelings.
2. Show empathy without condoning.
3. Share your feelings and perceptions.
4. Invite the child to focus on a solution.

When your child is engaging in a behavior based on a mistaken goal such as misguided power, begin by letting him know that you understand his feelings. Jamie displayed a variety of emotions, and Jack could have validated Jamie's feelings by showing empathy, by indicating that he understood what Jamie was feeling. Your display of empathy does not mean that you endorse the behaviors you are concerned about. Similarly, by showing empathy for Jamie's emotions related to cars (delight with having one and upset with having it taken away), Jack would not have been communicating that he approves of Jamie's intense focus on cars.

Remember That Your Child Will Listen to You After He Feels Listened To

Perhaps Jamie would have been more likely to listen to Jack's invitation and respond favorably to it had Jack listened to Jamie's messages. Finally, your child can be encouraged to help find a solution to avoid the problem in the future. Jack might have empowered Jamie to help find solutions that would diminish his focus on the car (e.g., by saying, "I have some puzzles we can play with. Where can you park the car while we play with the puzzles?"). An empowered child who is trusted to assist with generating solutions will more likely experience belonging and significance without engaging in behavior for the purpose of misguided power.

Use Family/Class Meetings

At home or in school, a meeting can be used as a time when children learn to give compliments to one another, to plan special events that will be shared together, and to generate positive solutions to problems. During family or class meetings, adults (parents or teachers) can model and promote cooperation. Children with special needs can learn to participate in meetings with family members at home or with the teacher and classmates at school. What is addressed at the meeting is, of course, dependent on the cognitive and communication abilities of the child participant(s). Given Jamie's age and developmental delays, a family meeting at his home would likely be short and simple. Planning special family events could be introduced in the early meetings. Teaching him the meaning and use of compliments could be added to later meetings. When he is capable of problem solving, this could be introduced into the agenda of the family meeting. Throughout these meetings with Jamie, the verbal messages communicated might be enhanced with visual displays (e.g., pictures drawn on a whiteboard, pictures of routines). Opportunities to connect with family or classmates on a regular basis at these special meetings have the potential to enhance a child's sense of belonging and significance. They can also assist a child in developing behaviors that make seeking misguided power unnecessary.

REVIEW OF POSITIVE DISCIPLINE TOOLS PRESENTED IN THIS CHAPTER

1. Make sure the message of love gets through.
2. Provide connection before correction.
3. Listen to "get into the child's world."
4. Reflect and/or validate feelings.
5. Take time for training.
6. Be kind and firm at the same time.
7. Follow the Three *R*s of recovery: Recognize, Reconcile, and Resolve.
8. Redirect your child to positive power by asking for help.
9. Offer limited choices.
10. Decide what you will do.
11. Let routines be the boss.
12. Follow the four steps for winning cooperation.
13. Hold family/class meetings.

RICKY'S STORY:
INFLUENCE YOUR CHILD'S
POTENTIAL

In the fall of 2005 a boy was born to a single mother living in a large metropolitan area. This boy, named Enrique, goes by Ricky. Ricky's mother, Andi, was sixteen years old when she gave birth to him. She had run away from home and was living on the streets when she became pregnant. She did not realize she was pregnant until her fourth month and had been using methamphetamines until then. When she learned that she was pregnant Andi called her mother and stepfather and asked if she could come home. Her boyfriend had just left her and she felt desperate.

Going home was not easy for Andi. She had run away during her sophomore year in high school because she was uncomfortable living under the rules her parents, Paula and Jim, had set for her. Andi's parents were at first overjoyed to see her. They had been very worried about her safety and health. Paula took her to a doctor so that Andi could have prenatal care for the last five months of her pregnancy.

For the first several weeks, Andi got along well with Paula and Jim even though they insisted that she return to school. Soon Andi became restless and made contact with some of her street friends. This had a negative effect on her school attendance and also led to renewed conflict with her parents. Andi resumed smoking cigarettes and drinking alcohol, although she did abstain from meth. Predictably, this state of affairs led to a confrontation with her parents. Andi's mother told her that she could stay at home only if she was willing to attend school regularly and give up tobacco, alcohol, and drugs. Andi agreed but continued to sneak away every once in a while.

When Ricky was born, Andi and her parents were overjoyed. Ricky was Paula and Jim's first grandchild and he was loved from his first moments of life. For the first month Andi dedicated herself to Ricky's care and Paula stayed in the background, really trying to let Andi be the mother. After that, Andi became restless again. She met a young man who encouraged her to "live a little" and have some fun. Andi began to let her mother provide more of Ricky's care. Paula confronted Andi and reminded her that she, Andi, was Ricky's mother and that he needed her. Filled with resentment, Andi stormed out with Ricky and moved in with her new boyfriend. She also quit high school.

Although Andi refused to let Paula know where she was living, she still brought Ricky around to spend time with his grandparents. Paula noticed signs that Ricky wasn't being adequately cared for. He was often dirty and his diaper unchanged when he arrived. He developed a runny nose that lasted for weeks. Finally, Andi left him with Paula and Jim for a weekend and did not return for over two weeks. When she came to pick him up, Andi appeared high to Paula, who refused to turn Ricky over. Andi screamed and berated her mother on the front lawn, finally stomping off. She returned the next day in much better shape and apologized to Paula. She admitted that she had been using meth but insisted that the fear of losing Ricky had made her see things more clearly. Afraid that she would lose contact with both of them, and against her better judgment, Paula sent Ricky home with Andi.

Paula did not hear from Andi or see Ricky for three weeks. Finally, she got a phone call from a panicked Andi, who pleaded with Paula to come and get her. When Paula arrived at the address Andi gave her, she found Andi huddled in a ball and shaking. Ricky was in a crib wailing. His diaper was full, and there were no diapers around to change him. The apartment was filled with garbage. In tears, Paula called paramedics and the police. Ricky was six months old.

For the next four and a half years Ricky lived with his grandparents. Andi was in and out of treatment centers, trying to give up her drug addiction. During this time Andi allowed her parental rights to be terminated and Ricky to be adopted by Paula and Jim. Andi remained in Ricky's life, but more as an "aunt" than a mother. Although her life continued to be unstable, she did manage to stay off drugs and alcohol. When Ricky was four, she had another baby, a girl named Malia. After Malia's birth Andi's life changed for the better. She got a job at a child-care center and was able to bring Malia with her. She moved into an apartment four blocks from her mother's house and continued to see Ricky frequently.

At age four Ricky was an angry little boy. Paula and Jim were worried about him, especially after he was asked to leave two child-care programs for extreme aggressive behavior toward other children. When an exasperated Paula scolded him for hurting other children, Ricky replied, "I don't care! I wanted *to hurt them!" Paula was afraid that he really meant it. After Ricky's second expulsion, Paula sought services from her local early childhood special education program. Ricky qualified for services and was placed in a social-skills preschool. Also at this time Paula brought Ricky in for a psychological assessment. After his history and current concerns were assessed, Ricky was believed to have a "disorganized attachment." Practically speaking, this meant that Ricky both craved and feared being close to the people who loved him. This is a serious condition that suggests that Ricky's ability to develop a secure attachment could be severely compromised.*

In the long-running debate between nature and nurture, Alfred Adler (Viennese psychiatrist and onetime colleague of Freud) came down somewhere in the sensible middle. He believed that children (and adults) are not hostages to either their biology or their early experiences. Both of these factors exert tremendous influence on children, but they are not all-powerful. Adler would argue that it isn't what children are born with or what they endure that is the ultimate determining factor in their lives. It is what they make of these experiences. As we have seen, children are constantly making decisions about what they need to do to thrive or survive. It is these decisions that determine their fate.

> Children are constantly making decisions about what they need to do to thrive or survive. It is these decisions that determine their fate.

As parents and teachers of children with special needs, you have the ability to be a positive influence on the decisions your child makes and ultimately on your child's potential, despite congenital conditions or traumatic experiences, either (or both) of which can lead to a special need. Toward that end, it is vital that parents and teachers do two important things. The first is to refrain from blaming children for the behaviors that are associated with their condition. When engaging in behaviors that are characteristic of the special condition, your child is acting with "innocence." The second is to take the time to teach children (in an encouraging way) alternatives to those behaviors.

As we saw with Courtney, the little girl with Down syndrome (in chapter 1), children make decisions all the time, often based on misinterpretations of their experiences. To fully flesh out this important point, it is necessary to make some important differentiations. Courtney and Hannah (in chapter 5) were born with certain conditions already present, Down syndrome and autism spectrum disorder. Ricky, as far as we know, was born neurotypical, that is, he did not have an identifiable and medically diagnosable condition at birth. (However, the fact that his mother used drugs and alcohol while pregnant is certainly a risk factor for him.) But all three of these children, at the age when we meet them, are children with special needs.

Courtney's and Hannah's special needs are a result of conditions they were born with. Ricky's condition, a disorganized attachment, by definition was set in motion (but not guaranteed) by a certain set of life experiences. As we will see when we further explore the concept of "innocent behaviors," this distinction is important. For now, it is enough to note that the set of behaviors that Ricky exhibits will be very difficult to consider innocent because they seem directed at others and especially at the people he loves and trusts the most. Courtney's innocent behaviors and, to a great extent, Hannah's innocent behaviors are more easily seen in the context of their respective conditions.

To put it in a more down-to-earth way, it will likely be easier for Courtney's mother to see that Courtney's difficulty in learning how to dress herself or her need for seemingly endless repetition to learn the simplest skills is not directed at her. It is almost always associated with having Down syndrome. On the other hand, Ricky's grandmother is likely to have a harder time seeing Ricky's rejecting behavior toward her as not directed at her. Knowing that this kind of behavior is directly related to his disorganized attachment does not necessarily make it easier for her when he screams, "I hate you! You're stupid! You're not my real mom!"

At preschool Ricky had a predictably rocky beginning. On his first day, he refused to come to circle time and stood watching. He seemed surprised when the teacher, Joel, told him that he was welcome to watch circle time and join the group when he was ready. When he came to the circle he refused to sit down. Again, his teacher did not argue; he said that standing was okay with him but that Ricky could sit if he changed his mind.

From this beginning Ricky made slow progress. He frequently, and loudly, refused to come to certain activities only to change his mind when Joel did not argue. (Joel did point out that certain parts of the room were unavailable but that no one was going to force Ricky to come to the activity that the group was doing.) Ricky also lashed out at other children, both with words and with his fists. Some of the time, his aggression "made sense," i.e., he hit or cussed when he didn't get his way or when another child had something he wanted. But at other times Ricky lashed out at other children seemingly unprovoked. When this happened, the teacher often found himself shaking his head, unable to believe that Ricky could be so hurtful with so little provocation. He removed Ricky from the group, but this only seemed to cause Ricky to escalate into a tantrum.

During one of these unprovoked occasions, Joel pointed out to Ricky that it hadn't seemed like the other child had done anything to him. He added that Ricky seemed pretty angry even before he hit the other child. Ricky responded, "I'm always mad." The teacher wondered out loud to Ricky whether there might be something sad underneath all that mad. Ricky did not answer.

From that point on, when Ricky was aggressive, his teacher would often begin their conversations by saying, "I know you're mad and sad a lot of the time. How can I help you now?" He would invite Ricky to consider solutions by showing him an "Anger Wheel of Choice" (figure 4) that had different alternatives to solve problems. As Ricky began to trust him more, Joel was able to intercede whenever Ricky hurt another child. In these situations, Joel asked Ricky what he thought might help that child. At first, Ricky had no idea. As time went on, he *might elect to apologize. On one occasion, he offered to save a prized red cup for the other child when he set the snack table!*

Ricky's teacher was able to penetrate Ricky's strong defenses by understanding (and making clear that he understood) that even when Ricky was hurting other people, he himself was feeling hurt. By addressing this crucial point, he was able to help Ricky to be gradually more open to problem solving.

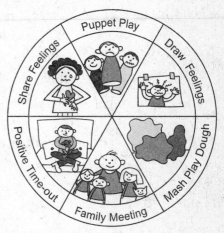

Figure 4. Anger Wheel of Choice.

Paula was very curious about how Ricky's teacher worked with him. One thing she noticed was that Ricky had fewer "meltdowns." With Joel's encouragement, Paula and Jim first read *Positive Discipline for Preschoolers* and then took a Positive Discipline parenting class. Admittedly, both felt a little sheepish, as they had successfully raised two of their three children and even Andi was now doing much better. They were pleasantly surprised not to be the only grandparents in the class as well as not the only parents of a very angry preschool child.

As the class progressed, Paula and Jim began to understand that, although Ricky had suffered a very traumatic first several months of life and was now demonstrating some very worrisome behaviors, his future was not already determined. They resolved that they would be positive and encouraging influences on him. Ricky did not make that easy.

> *One morning Ricky was watching cartoons before it was time to go to school. He had successfully ignored several requests from Jim to get his shoes on. Already somewhat angry at being ignored, Jim turned the television off and told Ricky in a very stern voice, "Get your shoes on RIGHT NOW!" Ricky reacted by dropping to the floor, kicking and screaming that he hated his grandfather. He then threw one of his shoes at Jim. Jim's first reaction was to yank Ricky to his feet.*

That's actually as far as Jim got down the "low road," as lessons from the book and class kicked in. He knew he was about to "flip his lid" (see chapter 3), and he remembered that Ricky's disorganized attachment often led him to "invite" rejection from people he loved.

> *Jim told Ricky in a soft voice that he thought they both needed to calm down. He then said that he was going to sit on the couch until he felt better, and he invited Ricky to join him. Ricky snarled and said, "No! I hate you! You're mean." Jim did not answer but just patted the couch beside him. After a minute or so, Ricky joined him, sitting stiffly. But he did not object when Jim put his arm around him. After a few silent moments Jim said, "You really wanted to keep watching cartoons." Ricky said nothing but snuggled a little closer. "You looked really mad when I turned the TV off. I'm sorry that I yelled at you." Ricky said, "Yeah, I love SpongeBob. And Patrick was being chased by a big squid." Jim smiled and said, "How about we look in the paper and see when it's on next and watch it together?" Ricky said, "Okay." Jim then said, "Now, though, I really need your help. School is starting soon and we both have to get ready. What could you do to help while I put away our breakfast dishes?" Ricky volunteered to let the dog out into the backyard and, when she came back in, to put his shoes on.*

Jim had decided as part of his growing understanding about Ricky that it was very important that he be a role model for the kind of person he believed Ricky could be. That included making mistakes and recovering from them. It also included getting feedback from Ricky when there was a problem to be solved. He found that Ricky was far less likely to balk when he was offered a say in the solution.

THE POSITIVE DISCIPLINE TOOLS RELATED TO INFLUENCING YOUR CHILD'S POTENTIAL

In order to influence your child's potential, despite whatever conditions he or she is either born with or acquires along the way, it is important that you both accept the fact that this condition exists *and* refuse to let this fact completely dominate your sense of your child's potential. The tools that will help you do these things are the following:

- Reflect and validate feelings.

- Take the time to teach.

- Work for improvement, not perfection.

- Use distraction and redirection.

- View mistakes as opportunities to learn.

After communicating to Ricky that he understood Ricky's emotional state by reflecting and validating his feelings, Joel took the time to help Ricky learn that there were alternatives to aggression when Ricky was confronted with a problem. He used the Anger Wheel of Choice as a visual way to represent options and did not push Ricky to choose any particular alternative. By not punishing or criticizing Ricky for reactions that were, in the short run, beyond his ability to control, the teacher helped Ricky make small gains. For example, by waiting until Ricky had developed a sense of trust before trying to help him see the social effects of his aggression on other children, Joel was working for gradual improvement over time.

At home, Ricky's grandparents were helping him as well. By owning his mistake of yelling at Ricky, Jim demonstrated that mistakes were acceptable and could even be fixed. To Ricky, the idea that he might be able to recover from a mistake (and that people would still love him) must have initially seemed quite foreign. In that same interaction, Jim very successfully used distraction to help Ricky, first by joining with him in his admiration of *SpongeBob* and then by suggesting that they check when they might watch together. He then used redirection to encourage Ricky to choose a way he might help in their joint process of getting ready for school.

THE POSITIVE DISCIPLINE TOOLS RELATED TO YOUR CHILD'S MISTAKEN GOAL

Once again, understanding the belief behind your child's behavior and the mistaken goal this belief leads him to pursue will be of immense value in helping your child experience a sense of belonging and significance. Ricky's teacher and grandfather both came to the same conclusion about Ricky's mistaken goal. They both noticed that when Ricky said or did something aggressive, their emotional reaction was frequently disbelief. "How could Ricky be so hurtful to his classmates?" Joel wondered. Jim, Ricky's grandfather, remarked to himself, "How can Ricky say such mean things to *me*?!" Both also noticed that when they responded simply to the hurting behavior, Ricky would almost always dramatically escalate. In their own ways, each understood Ricky's coded message: "I'm hurting. Validate my feelings." They saw Ricky's mistaken goal as revenge: "I don't think I belong, so I'll hurt others as I feel hurt. I can't be liked or loved."

> If revenge is your child's mistaken goal, you have no doubt already experienced the difficulty of responding to very hurtful behavior by first noticing how your child is hurting.

If revenge is your child's mistaken goal, you have no doubt already experienced the difficulty of responding to very hurtful behavior by first noticing how your child is hurting. There is something about a child being purposefully mean to another child or to us that makes us want to retaliate, perhaps because this behavior invites our own feelings of hurt, as well as our own mistaken goal of revenge. As was true with Ricky, however, retaliation usually leads to escalation. Instead, as difficult as it may sometimes seem, consider the Positive Discipline tools that follow.

Acknowledge Your Child's Hurt Feelings

When Jim realized that he had started to retaliate against Ricky for screaming at him and throwing a shoe, he regathered himself and made a statement to Ricky indicating that he understood that Ricky was angry at how Jim had abruptly turned off the television. It was helpful to Ricky to know that his grandfather "got it." When Ricky's teacher indicated that he understood that Ricky was "mad and sad a lot of the time," it was followed by an invitation to help.

Avoid Feeling Hurt

This is easier said than done. Jim had begun to react to his own feelings of being hurt when he remembered that it would be kinder and more helpful to Ricky to focus on Ricky. He was then able to engage Ricky in some problem solving that made both of them feel better. It is up to adults to break the "revenge cycle," since children do not have the maturity or skills to do so. Too often adults expect children to control their behavior when adults aren't controlling their own behavior.

> It is up to adults to break the "revenge cycle," since children do not have the maturity or skills to do so. Too often adults expect children to control their behavior when adults aren't controlling their own behavior.

Avoid Punishment and Retaliation

One aspect of Ricky's disorganized attachment (as well as of Ricky's mistaken belief about himself) is that he already believes that he is neither likeable nor lovable. This hurts and invites revenge from Ricky, so he hurts others. Both Joel and Jim went out of their way to avoid both punishment and retaliation and focused instead on encouragement by helping Ricky learn to solve problems as they came up.

Build Trust

Building trust, especially in a child who can seem so hostile and angry, is a long-term process. Yet each time Ricky's teacher acknowledges his feelings and helps him consider alternatives on the Anger Wheel of Choice, he builds a little trust. Each time Ricky's grandfather demonstrates his willingness to help Ricky work through difficult situations (and watches *SpongeBob* with him!) he builds a little more. Building trust is an important component of the Positive Discipline tool "connection before correction."

Use Reflective Listening

Reflective listening is listening in such a way as to make it clear that you really understand both what your child is saying and what he is feeling. It means listening between the words to what is meant as well as what is said. When Ricky was sitting next to his grandfather on the couch, silently sulking, Jim listened eloquently to that silence. First he made a statement that he understood how important it had been to Ricky to keep watching cartoons. This was followed by continued silence on Ricky's part, but with less sulking and more snuggling. Jim listened deeply to this also and made a comment about Ricky's anger at having the television shut off. This led the two of them to being able to solve the problem of how to get ready for school.

Make Amends

It might seem backward to make amends to someone who has been hurtful to you or someone else. However, taking responsibility for our own behavior is a powerful teaching tool for our children. How many times have we heard that experience is the best teacher? Jim made amends in his interaction with Ricky by apologizing for yelling at Ricky and by making a plan with him to watch *SpongeBob* together at a different time (when they weren't getting ready for school). Over time, Ricky's teacher was teaching Ricky to make amends when he had hurt another child.

> Taking responsibility for our own behavior is a powerful teaching tool for our children.

This is also a good time to make the point that children do not learn the value of apologies by being made to apologize. A sincere apology can be a very powerful and healing experience between two people, but the key word there is "sincere." A child can be made to say "I'm sorry," but not to mean it. Sincere apologies are learned over time when children experience us, their teachers and parents, taking responsibility and making amends. Children sometimes come to their own conclusion about making an apology when they are asked what they think might help the other child feel better. When it is their idea, the apology is usually sincere.

Show You Care

Remember: Children pursuing the mistaken goal of revenge believe that they are neither likeable nor lovable. Gestures small and large that communicate

> A child can be made to say "I'm sorry," but not to mean it.

that you do indeed care for and about them are very powerful. Jim communicated his caring by his validation of Ricky's feelings, by his admission of his own mistakes, by his silent invitation to Ricky to join him on the couch, by his arm around Ricky's angry and sullen shoulders, and by his invitation for them to spend some special time together.

Use Positive Time-out

We know from chapter 3 that no one can effectively engage in solving problems when his or her "lid is flipped." (There is a more extensive discussion of positive time-out in chapter 4.) Jim was demonstrating to Ricky how to take a positive time-out by telling him that he was going to sit on the couch until he felt better. At home, Jim and Paula might want to have Ricky help them designate a space for positive time-out, somewhere that Ricky can go and help himself feel better until he is ready to help find a solution. At school Ricky's teacher might consider getting the whole class involved in setting up a similar space.

Use Family and Class Meetings

As we have suggested, family and class meetings are useful for a host of reasons. For a child who already believes that he does not belong and is not important, family and class meetings can be a graphic illustration of the reverse. Meetings call attention to the fact that all of the people who attend, children and adults, are part of the family or class. Children learn to listen to one another and to respect different points of view. They learn the skill of brainstorming for solutions and choosing one that is respectful to everyone. Each person in the meetings has a unique and important role to play. This helps children develop a sense of belonging and significance and thus decreases their need to find belonging and significance through misbehavior (a mistaken goal).

REVIEW OF POSITIVE DISCIPLINE TOOLS PRESENTED IN THIS CHAPTER

1. Reflect and validate feelings.
2. Take time to teach.
3. Work for improvement, not perfection.
4. Use distraction and redirection.
5. View mistakes as opportunities to learn.
6. Acknowledge your child's hurt feelings.
7. Avoid feeling hurt.
8. Avoid punishment and retaliation.
9. Build trust.
10. Use reflective listening.
11. Make amends.
12. Show you care.
13. Use positive time-out.
14. Use family and class meetings.

BENJY'S STORY:
GET INTO YOUR CHILD'S WORLD

It was "art time" in Benjy's early childhood special education preschool class, and all the four-year-olds flocked around the art table, reaching for available brushes and sponges to dip into the colorful paints or just immersing their small hands in the vibrant, thick liquid and smearing it on the paper in front of them. That is, all the preschoolers except Benjy. When he heard the word art, *unlike the majority of his classmates, who hustled over to the little art corner of the classroom to see what inviting materials their teacher had set out for them, Benjy moved quickly to another part of the classroom. When encouraged by an instructor to join the art activity, Benjy usually made no eye contact and proceeded to find a toy of interest to play with. The staff in Benjy's current classroom (for children on the autism spectrum) had learned from his previous instructors that he had an intense dislike for art. In his previous preschool, when a teacher led him by the hand or carried him to the art table after he had shown his reluctance to accompany her, Benjy's usual response was gagging followed by a temper tantrum. His tantrums usually included screaming and crying, falling to the floor, and flailing his arms and legs. His current preschool staff avoided leading or carrying him to the art corner, as they did not want to invite such an extreme reaction. Even when they merely told him that it was art time, or showed him the art project for the day and a schedule picture that represented art time, Benjy usually pushed the picture or the art items away and retreated from his teacher. He often started to gag at the sight of art materials (especially paints, glue, and play dough) whenever these were shown to him.*

Benjy's preschool teacher, Lilly, trained as a specialist in early intervention and early childhood special education, felt conflicted about his lack of participation in art time. On the one hand, she believed that, considering his significant delays in all areas of development, there were many other skills that she could teach him, thus replacing the goal of "exploring a variety of art media" with a goal more crucial for his long-term survival. On the other hand, she knew that Benjy was a candidate for the developmental kindergarten in his progressive district for the coming school year and that his school district's special education team wanted him to be able to participate in all kindergarten activities, including art time. Because Benjy would be exposed to art on a regular basis in his kindergarten program, Lilly wanted to help him find some joy in this activity. Having just attended the Positive Discipline in the Classroom two-day workshop, she decided to use the Positive Discipline concept of "getting into the child's world" as her guide to help Benjy get ready for his kindergarten program.

Each child with (or without) special needs is truly unique and distinct from any other child. Labels are used in special education and medicine to categorize children for many purposes, such as determining their eligibility for services, deciding what educational method or treatment protocol might be useful in helping them, or assigning them to specific groups in a research study. However useful labels might be for these purposes, they cannot disguise the fact that each child with special needs has particular likes and dislikes, a temperament unique to her, and an individual profile of strengths and weaknesses in important areas of development that is not identical to that of any other child. Therefore, when trying to decide what will be helpful for your child, it is critical that you understand, as much as you can, what the world looks like through her eyes. What does she like and dislike? What is her unique temperament? What is she especially good at and what does she struggle with? As you make new discoveries about your child, you will better understand her distinct point of view. This understanding will, in turn, help you to know how to help her learn important skills and how to respond to her respectfully when she experiences challenges.

> When trying to decide what will be helpful for your child, it is critical that you understand, as much as you can, what the world looks like through her eyes.

When Lilly learned about Benjy's upcoming placement in her group, she first read his evaluation reports and Individualized Family Service Plan, talked to his parents and previous teacher, and observed him in his preschool group designed for children with developmental delays. These were useful sources of information because they helped her to learn about Benjy from the perspective of those who had spent all his life with him and knew him best (his parents) and those who had focused in detail on his special education needs (his evaluation team and previous teacher). After he started attending her class, Lilly began to know him more personally by learning firsthand about his likes and dislikes, his temperament, and his strengths and learning challenges. This enabled her to respond to his refusal to join art time by getting into his world in an effort to understand his experiences from his point of view, and to make decisions about how to assist him. Positive Discipline offers many tools that help parents and teachers *understand and get into the child's world.*

POSITIVE DISCIPLINE TOOLS FOR GETTING INTO YOUR CHILD'S WORLD

The Positive Discipline tools for understanding and getting into your child's world are numerous. These respectful tools are invaluable whenever you begin assisting your child in overcoming a challenge. They include the following:

- Understand your child's uniqueness by . . .
    - knowing your child's likes and dislikes.

    - appreciating your child's temperament.

    - recognizing your child's strengths and learning challenges.

- Get into your child's world by . . .
    - empathizing with your child and validating feelings.

    - "listening" with more than just your ears.

    - asking curiosity questions.

    - giving special time.

    - providing connection before correction.

- Recognize that mistakes are opportunities to learn.

Know Your Child's Likes and Dislikes

Benjy's teacher, through her consultation with his occupational therapist, learned that he exhibited "sensory defensiveness" across a wide range of daily activities. To understand sensory defensiveness, we will briefly describe the relationship between sensory experience and the brain. Our senses (what we see, hear, touch, taste, and smell, as well as how we experience movement and gravity) take in information, and our brains process and integrate the important information and filter out what we don't need. Some children can be overly sensitive to certain kinds of sensory stimulation, for example, those who are terrified by the sound of a vacuum cleaner or can't stand the radio turned up and those who are driven crazy by the tags in the backs of their shirts or by shoelaces tied too loose or too tight. Their brains are not filtering properly, making it very hard for these children to concentrate on the things they need to concentrate on. And that sensitivity can grate on them to such an extent that they don't seem to have patience for small upsets. (Their sensory systems are already upset!) Sensory defensiveness occurs when these children interpret sensory stimulation as unpleasant and react to it with avoidance and often aversion to the sensory experience. Children with sensory defensiveness can be easily overwhelmed or even disgusted by what they take in through their senses. Sounds or smells, for example, that other children experience as routine may lead these children to have an aversive reaction.[7]

As a result of his sensory defensiveness, Benjy greatly disliked activities that involved touching, smelling, or even seeing items that were in the form of thick liquids with an odor, such as paints and glue. Further, he showed an aversive reaction to sitting on certain types of seats in the classroom. He disliked sitting on chairs with a hard surface and preferred seating with a soft cushion (e.g., beanbag chair, padded chair, mini trampoline). It is important to note that for Benjy this was more than a matter of preference. His tactile sense was thrown off kilter by activities that he registered as unpleasant, which made participating in these activities uncomfortable for him.

Benjy had a small repertoire of items that he cared about. He liked playing with small, solid toys that he could hold in his hands and preferred having at least two of the same toy, one for each hand. Little balls and cars were among his favorites; he enjoyed holding, releasing, and watching them as they moved.

Given these likes and dislikes, Lilly decided to introduce him to marble art, initially without the paint. She placed two shiny silver marbles inside the 1½-inch lid of a file box. While Benjy's classmates were involved at the art table, she presented the lid with marbles to him while he was playing with toys on the therapy mat. Having not yet introduced marbles to Benjy in the preschool classroom, she was pleased to see that he enjoyed watching the two little marbles roll around inside the lid as she tilted it back and forth. The next day, prior to presenting Benjy with the box lid containing the two marbles, Lilly placed a very small dot (⅛ teaspoon) of odor-free paint on a piece of construction paper that she had placed inside the lid. Benjy didn't seem to notice the paint initially as his eyes followed the random movement of the shiny marbles. He continued to watch the movement of the marbles with interest even as they began to make tiny streaks of color on the paper and became slightly covered in paint. During the weeks that followed, Lilly engaged him in art by using the marble art materials to introduce new and different things. He was given his "marble art template" with variations in color of paint, amount of paint (up to half a teaspoon), size and type of rolling toy, and designs on the construction paper. The box lid with contents was always prepared for him in advance to spare him the unpleasant experience of observing paint being squeezed onto the paper. By understanding Benjy's uniqueness through her knowledge of his likes and dislikes, Lilly was able to successfully introduce him to an art activity. Moreover, she used his growing familiarity and comfort with one thing to help him try something new and different.

If you are trying to teach your child a new skill and she resists your efforts, try to understand this reluctance by considering her unique likes and dislikes. Is there some feature of the task that she finds unpleasant? Can this be reasonably diminished? Could the task be modified to make it more tolerable or even pleasant for her? Is there a way to embed something she likes into the task you are teaching? From her perspective, the new skill you are introducing will be more interesting if it's related to something she likes and contains little trace of what she greatly dislikes.

Appreciate Your Child's Temperament

In their longitudinal study, Drs. Stella Chess and Alexander Thomas discovered nine major qualities related to a child's temperament.[8] A temperament is a pattern of traits or qualities that describes a person. This combination of traits influences each person's unique personality. All children demonstrate varying degrees of each of the nine qualities outlined by Chess and Thomas. These include the following:

1. Activity level: the child's motor activity level and the amount of time spent being active as opposed to being inactive

2. Rhythmicity: the degree of predictability of biological functions such as hunger, sleep, and bowel movements

3. Initial response: the way a child reacts to new people, objects, situations, or places, either positively or negatively

4. Adaptability: the child's long-term reaction to changes in her life, such as quick adaptability or a lengthier amount of time needed to adjust

5. Sensory threshold: the level of sensitivity a child shows to sensory input

6. Quality of mood: the child's overall disposition—pleasant and content, or unpleasant and discontent

7. Intensity of reactions: the amount of energy that a child displays when she responds to a situation

8. Distractibility: the degree to which an outside stimulus can interfere with the child's ongoing actions

9. Persistence and attention span: the child's ability to maintain engagement with an activity despite difficulties and the length of engagement in an activity without interruption

Through her experiences with Benjy, Lilly discovered that he tended to spend more time inactive than active. His parents reported that his eating and sleeping patterns were unpredictable. He was usually slow to warm up to anything or anyone new to him, and it took him considerable time to adjust to a new change. As mentioned earlier, Benjy was highly sensitive to certain things, and this was especially true in terms of how these things felt, smelled, tasted, or looked to him. His mood was overall more serious than cheerful, and it could change very quickly from expressions of extreme delight to dramatic displeasure. His affect in most contexts was subdued; however, some situations elicited an intense reaction from him. His distractibility, persistence, and attention were all relative to the context. While he was able to focus for long periods of time, without distraction, on activities of high interest to him, he showed very limited attention and persistence, accompanied by considerable distractibility, during activities that seemed to not interest him.

By learning about his temperament and appreciating his unique way of being in the world, Lilly learned to respectfully plan and adjust her instruction for him. Because he was slow to warm up to novel situations and took a long time to integrate a change, she modified his art activities ever so slightly over the course of many weeks. She greatly reduced the sensory input that made him uncomfortable and also did not require that he complete his project at the art table where he could see and smell items that were unpleasant for him. Also, she helped him to sustain his attention to the art activity by including high-interest items in his marble art template.

When you are trying to help your child overcome a challenge, consider the nine traits related to your child's temperament. By understanding your child's unique temperament, you will gain ideas and insights that will help you make more informed decisions about how to help your child tolerate difficult situations.

Recognize Your Child's Strengths and Learning Challenges

All children with special needs have strengths and learning challenges. In special education, these are referred to as "strengths and weaknesses." The child's strengths and learning challenges are important to identify in order to develop the goals for her annual educational plan (Individualized Family Service Plan or Individualized Education Plan). As you learn more about your child's particular strengths and challenges, you will be in a better position both to help her learn and to advocate for her needs in the educational system.

Although your child has special needs, it may also be true that she has a special talent or two. For example, the child with the label of "ADHD" (attention-deficit/hyperactivity disorder) may be intellectually gifted in some areas of development. The child with the label of "ASD" (autism spectrum disorder) may show a precocious talent in a certain subject area. A child given the label of "mentally retarded" may demonstrate a special and noteworthy skill compared to his overall global delays in development. While this book uses the still common term "mental retardation," we should note that the field of special education now uses the more accurate term "intellectual disability."

Lilly was aware of the many areas in which Benjy was challenged. He did not use words or signs to communicate, and his use of individual picture symbols was just beginning to emerge. He needed help from others to get dressed and undressed, to use utensils during meals, to bathe and toilet himself, and to carry out virtually all other activities of daily living. His movements were slow and somewhat uncoordinated, and he needed help with climbing and riding a tricycle. He was hesitant to interact with people outside his family, and although he liked to watch other children, he did not attempt to play with them.

Yet in spite of Benjy's learning challenges, Lilly paid very close attention to his areas of strength so that she could make the most of these whenever possible. For example, he had an unusual attentiveness to numbers and alphabet letters even though he had not been formally exposed to them. He picked out particular numbers from puzzle boards and stared at wall displays that contained these favorite numbers. When he was not actively playing with a toy, Lilly often observed him staring at the wall clock or the display of large alphabet letters (in sequence) on the wall above the circle-time area. She knew that he was paying attention to the numbers and letters exhibited because when she began singing the alphabet song or a number song at the time he was focusing on letters or numbers, he usually began smiling and gazing from her eyes to the wall display and back again, demonstrating that he was making reference to the same shared experience.

Lilly was able to use his interest in numbers and letters to assist him with attending to and participating in art. The design on the construction paper inside his marble art template often included numbers or alphabet letters. So it was not only the movement of the balls rolling inside the box lid that maintained his attention to the art activity; it was also the visual design on the paper inside the lid that captured and sustained his attention. In addition, Lilly counted to ten slowly and musically or sang the alphabet song as she rocked the box lid back and forth. Because he had a strong and positive association with hearing numbers and letters, this audible accompaniment to his art activity usually brought a smile to his face. Separate from art, Lilly discovered that simple picture board books with a number or letter displayed on each page were quite helpful in pleasurably exposing Benjy to books. Prior to this he had not shown any interest in books at all.

By integrating your child's strengths, talents, or unusual abilities into an activity designed to help him acquire a skill that is challenging for him, you positively and respectfully support his learning. Further, by recognizing your child's personal profile of strengths and learning challenges, you will better understand the unique perspective that he brings to a learning situation.

> By integrating your child's strengths, talents, or unusual abilities into an activity designed to help him acquire a skill that is challenging for him, you positively and respectfully support his learning.

Empathize with Your Child and Validate Feelings

Empathizing with your child will help you to get into her world. When you empathize with your child, you are communicating by your words, tone of voice, facial expression, and other body language the message *I understand what it is like to be you in this moment.* Essentially, when you validate your child's feelings, she *"feels felt."*[9] Words that you can use with your child to convey your empathic concern include any of the following: "You seem ____," "You look ____," "You sound ____," "You are ____." Basic feeling words can be inserted in the statement. For young children, these include the following: *happy, sad, mad, scared, frustrated, excited, tired, proud, sick, silly, disappointed,* and *worried.* For older children, you can consider a more advanced vocabulary of feelings.

Some children with special needs are more attentive to the feeling words in your empathic statements if you also show them pictures of the feelings. Especially for a child who has a limited understanding of words, a picture of the feeling that she is experiencing can immediately communicate to her that you understand her world at that moment. It is also a way for children to start learning that this sensation in her body has a name. Children who have words for their feelings, even if they have to rely on picture cards to communicate them, have less need to act these feelings out.

Be aware, however, that the timing of your empathic remark and presentation of the feeling picture is critical for some children. When your child is displaying intense behaviors during a meltdown, your first priority is to keep her and others around her safe. Your reference to how she feels at the height of her temper tantrum may provoke her even more. Keep in mind what we have learned about brain development: No one does her best problem solving with a "flipped lid." Since each child will respond differently to your statements of empathy, take note of when these are most helpful to share. At times, it is best to send "energetic empathy." This could mean sitting close by with a feeling of empathy that is communicated through your positive energy instead of your words. Your body language, including eye gaze, facial expression, gestures, and body orientation, will enhance the message of empathy that you feel for your child.

As you validate your child's feelings, avoid trying to talk your child out of her feelings (e.g., commenting, "You're okay"), to fix her feelings (e.g., saying, "Be happy"), or to rescue your child from her feelings (e.g., taking the toy she wants from her sister when her sister is not ready to give it up). Sharing energetic empathy is a good way for you to learn to keep your mouth shut when it is appropriate to do so. When you empathize with your child without trying to change the way she feels, you let her know that you understand what she's going through and show faith in her ability to cope with her feelings. You are doing your child a great service when you teach her, through your empathy, to recognize her feelings, which is her first step to learning self-management.

> For a child who has a limited understanding of words, a picture of the feeling that she is experiencing can immediately communicate to her that you understand her world at that moment. It is also a way for a child to start learning that this sensation in her body has a name.

You are doing your child a great service when you teach her, through your empathy, to recognize her feelings, which is her first step to learning self-management.

Benjy had a small vocabulary of single words that he consistently understood. Hence, when Lilly empathized with him during pleasant and unpleasant situations, she exposed him to a number of important feeling words. She accompanied her spoken words of empathy with a picture of his feeling. For example, when Benjy showed signs of happiness, she empathized by showing a picture depicting "happy" while saying, "You are happy!" And when he was frustrated about something, she validated his feelings by saying, "You are frustrated!" while showing the picture of "frustrated." It is noteworthy that a picture seemed to catch Benjy's attention more than the audible word. In fact, the opportunity to gaze at a picture that portrayed his feeling, especially during an unpleasant situation, began to calm him. By validating what Benjy was feeling, and by communicating her understanding of his feeling through the use of both word and picture, Lilly was helping him to begin learning how to cope with his unpleasant feelings.

"Listen" with More Than Just Your Ears

Children with special needs show a broad continuum of communication abilities. They vary from those who are able to speak and communicate like other children their age to those who are so significantly delayed that they are able to use neither words nor conventional nonverbal forms of communication such as sign language, picture communication boards, or electronic communication devices. Regardless of your child's communication competence, listening to her by hearing the words she says as well as "listening" to what she is communicating, using more than your ears, will help you to get into her world and gain an understanding of life from her point of view.

Regardless of your child's communication competence, listening to her by hearing the words she says as well as "listening" to what she is communicating, using "more than your ears," will help you to get into her world and gain an understanding of life from her point of view.

Listening with more than your ears requires using your eyes to see her facial expression, her body posture, her body orientation, the speed of her movements, the direction and focus of her gaze, her gestures, and other aspects of her body language. Listening with more than your ears entails using your own sensations of touch and movement when you are in close physical proximity to her to feel her body's level of energy, from slow and weak to quick and strong. Listening with more than your ears, without judgment and for the purpose of trying to know what it's like to be in her body at any given moment, will greatly assist you in getting into your child's world. From the vantage point of understanding her world better, you can more flexibly and creatively consider solutions to challenges that will work for both her and you. If this all sounds complicated and challenging to you, you're right. It is! We all spend our whole lives learning to communicate better and better. Will you make mistakes? Yes. Will you and your child recover from them? Also yes. Remember the Three *R*s of Recovery! (See page 38.)

Because Benjy did not use any words to communicate, nor did he use sign language or picture symbols to express himself, Lilly regularly listened to him with more than her ears. On the basis of what she "heard," she could adjust many aspects of her instruction to him in order to remove unnecessary challenges in an activity or minimize the amount of challenge in an activity in order to make the activity more achievable for him. It is important to note here that Lilly did not try to eliminate challenges for Benjy, but rather tried to make them within his reach if he stretched.

For example, when he was learning how to eat a variety of foods at snack time, Lilly didn't require that he sit at the snack table on a regular preschool-size chair, as did the other children in his group. His unhappy facial expression combined with his physical avoidance of the typical preschool chairs informed his teacher that seating like this was challenging to his sensory system. "Hearing" this message, she permitted him to eat his snack while sitting in a padded car seat, which he took to very readily. Thus, she eliminated an unnecessary challenge for him: sitting in a chair that he found uncomfortable. In the absence of this challenge, he was able to focus on eating.

In another example, he showed reluctance, through facial expression and bodily resistance, to leave the mini trampoline where he was sitting comfortably and playing with toys. If the activity he was requested to join was circle time with his classmates (who were all sitting on preschool chairs), he was permitted to stay on the mini trampoline, which Lilly pulled closer to the circle area. His proximity to the circle area enabled him to be more attentive to the circle-time activities. At the same time, he experienced a reduced amount of challenge joining circle time because he was allowed to continue sitting on the trampoline. By minimizing but not eliminating the challenges he faced when asked to join circle time, Lilly was able to help him be more successful in attending to and participating in the group circle activities.

Ask Curiosity Questions

Asking your child questions that invite her to think about solutions for a challenge she faces is another Positive Discipline tool for getting into her world. By asking curiosity questions and listening to her responses, you increase your ability to see the problem from your child's point of view (and not just your own) and you assist her in developing the ability to be a problem solver.

Just as with the "listening" tool described above, you will need to adjust your curiosity questions to the communication level of your child. Both what she understands and how she expresses herself will determine the level of complexity of your questions. Children with more communication ability will be able to understand "what" and "how" curiosity questions, such as "What do you need for . . . ?" or "How can you . . . ?" Children with significantly less communication ability show through their actions how they perceive a problem; they can be invited to problem-solve a solution through minimal words and gestures.

For example, Benjy was learning to put toys in a box after he finished playing with them. Lilly provided him with assistance because he could not accomplish this task on his own. She placed her hand on top of his hand and gently guided him to pick up the toys he had been playing with and place them inside a box. After many weeks of this type of assistance, Lilly began to reduce the amount of help she gave him, as he began to do some of the actions on his own. Occasionally, he picked up the toy and then accidentally dropped the toy outside the box without seeming to notice his mistake. Rather than pick up the toy for him, Lilly exclaimed in a cheerful tone of voice, "Oops!" then pointed to the toy that had fallen, and waited for his response. Her use of one word followed by a gesture and purposeful pause led him to notice the problem (the fallen toy) and generate a solution (picking it up again and placing it in the box). Lilly's style of problem-solving a solution with Benjy through the use of minimal words and gestures formed the foundation for later, more advanced problem solving for him, which could include a curiosity question such as "What can you do?"

Give Special Time

When you schedule regular special time with your child, you are using a Positive Discipline tool that will help nurture and support a long-term mutually respectful, loving relationship with your child. Also, giving your child special time will have the added benefit of assisting you in getting into your child's world so that you can gain insights about how to help her deal with challenges when they arise.

Benjy was given considerable special time in his early childhood special education preschool. Because of his significant delays in development, there were very few preschool skills that he could accomplish on his own. During the majority of his class time, he received specialized support from Lilly or from one of her assistants. Benjy showed warmth and interest in the adults who gave him special time, and in turn, the adults who spent the most time with him felt a loving connection with him. During their special time with Benjy, Lilly and her assistants became more alert to signs of his unique perspective and could generate solutions to challenges with him based on what they came to hypothesize about his point of view. By giving Benjy special time on a regular basis, his instructors were able to get into his world and provide more individualized help when he experienced challenges.

Create a Connection Before Correction

Another Positive Discipline tool that will help you to get into your child's world is "connection before correction." If you wish to provide corrective feedback to your child for a mistake she has made, engage with her in a kind and loving way before correcting her. Get close to her and down to her eye level so she feels your connection and sees that you're addressing her. Speak in a regular volume and in a neutral or cheerful tone of voice. What's most important in the use of this tool is that the message of love get through and that your child feel your love for her as much as or more than she feels your concern about the mistake she has made.

Because Benjy required considerable adult guidance to accomplish many tasks, he often needed corrective feedback for the innocent mistakes he made when attempting to carry out a task on his own. Benjy's instructors viewed his mistakes as opportunities for him to learn. They also saw his mistakes as opportunities for them to learn how to do a better job of providing him with the support he needed and of not reducing their supportive assistance too quickly. Overall, his instructors interacted with Benjy in a warm and upbeat fashion. They believed that maintaining a loving and supportive relationship with him was a top priority and that correction would be helpful to him only in the context of a loving connection.

When you use the nine Positive Discipline tools described above for understanding and getting into your child's world, you will discover that you are able to respond to the challenges you face with your child with greater understanding and increased flexibility. In addition, used on a regular basis with your child, these tools will form the foundation of a relationship built on closeness, trust, and mutual respect.

> These tools, used on a regular basis with your child, will form the foundation of a relationship built on closeness, trust, and mutual respect.

THE POSITIVE DISCIPLINE TOOLS RELATED TO YOUR CHILD'S MISTAKEN GOAL

In addition to the nine Positive Discipline tools for understanding and getting into your child's world, you can use Positive Discipline tools to help your child whenever she engages in misguided behaviors. Through your understanding of the mistaken belief behind your child's misguided behavior, you can select tools for responding in proactive and encouraging ways based on his mistaken goal. The art-time scenario above provides a brief description of the intensity of Benjy's temper tantrums when they had occurred in his previous preschool. The following scenario illuminates how a brief interaction with Benjy by his new teacher, Lilly, invited such a significant temper tantrum.

> It was "choice time" shortly after the preschoolers arrived, and the children were encouraged to choose toys to play with. Benjy was sitting on the carpet manipulating the colored wooden rings of a ring tower. Instead of placing the rings on the wooden pole, he repeatedly rolled the rings on the floor in front of him and watched them as they fell over. Lilly, his teacher, concerned that he was engaging in repetitive, self-stimulatory behavior rather than playing with the toy in a more productive way, seated herself on the carpet across from Benjy. She offered assistance by gently guiding his hand to pick up a ring and place it on the tower. Benjy resisted her help, and Lilly, feeling somewhat challenged by his resistance, continued to physically guide his hand. In a split second, without a moment's notice, Benjy shoved her hand away with a mighty force, began to scream, fell backward onto the floor, and then thrust his legs out in front of him, accidentally kicking the wooden rings across the floor. His tantrum lasted at least five minutes. Because Lilly had recently learned the principles and tools of Positive Discipline, she recognized immediately that Benjy's tantrum was provoked by how she had interacted with him, engaging in a power struggle. She gained considerable insight into Benjy's behavior through that one brief encounter with him, and never again during an interaction with her did Benjy have a meltdown!

Understand Innocent Behavior and Avoid Mistaken Interpretation

Before we analyze the mistaken goal related to Benjy's temper tantrum, a refresher about innocent behavior and mistaken interpretation is in order. Behaviors associated with the child's handicapping condition are "innocent" and require educational and therapeutic interventions. If we misinterpret a child's innocent behavior, reacting as if the child were deliberately "misbehaving," then there's a risk that the innocent behavior itself will become directed at us and/or new challenging behavior will be elicited in response to being made to stop the innocent behavior.

> If we misinterpret a child's innocent behavior, reacting as if the child were deliberately "misbehaving," then there's a risk that the innocent behavior itself will become directed at us and/or new challenging behavior will be elicited in response to being "made" to stop the innocent behavior.

Benjy's repetitive rolling of the wooden rings was innocent behavior, just as gagging at the sight of certain art materials with specific sensory properties was innocent behavior. Both types of behavior were associated with his handicapping condition. In addition, his physical resistance to being taken by his teacher to the art area and his physical resistance to having his hand guided through the motions of stacking rings on the pole were innocent behaviors. Without words, hand signs, or any other symbolic means for communicating *No, thank you, I don't want your help,* Benjy's physical resistance was his only means of conveying this message. His physical resistance to an adult's physical prompting was his only socially acceptable form of refusal and was associated with his significant delay in communication. When Lilly did not respectfully "listen" to his refusal, but instead mistakenly interpreted the resistance as "misbehavior" and continued to move his hand through the action of stacking rings, Benjy's innocent behavior was transformed into mistaken-goal behavior. The mistaken goal of Benjy's temper tantrum was misguided power. He communicated through his actions, loud and clear, *You can't make me!*

Having immediately recognized what she had provoked in Benjy by not listening to his nonverbal message of physical resistance, Lilly instantly responded with Positive Discipline tools that helped him feel a sense of belonging and significance and that helped her to more accurately frame her interpretation of his innocent behavior.

Tools That Mitigate the Goal of Misguided Power

There are many Positive Discipline tools that that can be considered when misguided power is a child's mistaken goal. The ones that Benjy's teacher immediately used were the following:

- Acknowledge that you can't force him.
- Withdraw from the conflict.
- Communicate love and caring.
- Redirect to positive power.

Lilly learned that she could not force Benjy to stack rings on the pole, nor could she manually guide him to carry out any other action if he was not willing to be assisted in carrying out the action. She learned not to guide his hand to complete an activity if he physically resisted her efforts, and she therefore withdrew from engaging in conflict with him. On the one occasion that he had a temper tantrum, she waited quietly, calmly, and patiently as he screamed, flailed, and rolled on the floor. Through her silent, serene, and undemanding manner, she communicated energetically her caring and compassion for him. When he finally calmed down completely, she redirected him to use his power positively through joining one of his classmates in a playful tug-of-war, which he greatly enjoyed. Through this experience, Lilly gained increased understanding of Benjy's innocent behavior and learned not to take it personally. Also, she discovered that when she incorrectly interpreted the motive for Benjy's behavior and inadvertently provoked his temper tantrum, she could use Positive Discipline tools to help Benjy recover from her error.

REVIEW OF POSITIVE DISCIPLINE TOOLS PRESENTED IN THIS CHAPTER

1. Understand your child's uniqueness by . . .

    a. knowing your child's likes and dislikes.

    b. appreciating your child's temperament.

    c. recognizing your child's strengths and learning challenges.

2. Get into your child's world by . . .

    a. empathizing with your child and validating her feelings.

    b. "listening" with more than just your ears.

    c. asking curiosity questions.

    d. giving special time.

    e. providing connection before correction.

3. Understand your child's innocent behavior.

4. Avoid mistaken interpretation of your child's behavior.

5. Recognize that mistakes are opportunities to learn.

6. Acknowledge that you can't force your child.

7. Withdraw from the conflict.

8. Communicate love and caring.

9. Redirect to positive power.

NATALYA'S STORY:
PROVIDE OPPORTUNITIES FOR
SOCIAL CONNECTION AND
CONTRIBUTION

Seven-year-old Natalya spent the first two years of her life in an orphanage on the outskirts of Moscow. Nothing is known about her parents, as she literally was left on the doorstep of the orphanage when she was only about a month old. A physical examination showed her to be in reasonably good health, although she was extremely small for what her age was thought to be. Not much is known about her life in the orphanage, either, except that the orphanage itself was always both crowded and understaffed.

At age two Natalya was adopted by an American family. She

became the youngest of three children in the household. Her new big brother was five years old and her new big sister was eight. Everyone in the McKenzie family seemed delighted with the tiny blond-haired and blue-eyed toddler.

At first, when Natalya ate everything she could get her hands on, Mr. and Mrs. McKenzie attributed it to the likely deprivation Natalya had experienced both before and at the orphanage. Likewise, when she continually grabbed toys away from both of her siblings, her parents, remembering the other children's "terrible twos," ascribed it to her level of development: unpleasant but not unexpected.

As time went by, Natalya learned to understand and speak English quite well. In fact, her parents were pleased with and impressed by how verbal she had become. Natalya's appetite also moderated. But her inability to share only became more pronounced. In fact, by age three and a half, Natalya was having multiple and prolonged tantrums daily, seemingly whenever she had to give something up, take turns, or simply wait. When in the throes of one of these tantrums, Natalya lashed out at anyone she could reach. All of the other family members received some bruising.

These intense tantrums took their toll on the family. Even with help from a family therapist, the emotional atmosphere of the household worsened. The McKenzie parents saw the effects of this ongoing strain on their other children and felt brokenhearted. When Natalya was four and a half, the McKenzies, with much heartache, relinquished their parental rights. The adoption was disrupted and Natalya was placed in foster care.

Over the course of the next three years, Natalya lived in three foster homes. In the first two, her behavior proved too challenging. In both of these homes, the parents became so discouraged that they resorted to punishing Natalya by taking away possessions and privileges when she adamantly refused to share anything and became aggressive in response to any attempt to intervene with her. They also, in violation of state regulations for foster parents, spanked her for what they referred to as her "mean behavior" toward the other children. At age seven, Natalya was in her fourth American home. These foster parents were struggling with her too.

During the course of her odyssey, Natalya had been taken to see numerous doctors and therapists, the last of whom had given her a diagnosis of oppositional defiant disorder. Much to her good fortune, however, Natalya had a caseworker at the state Department of Human Services who refused to give up on her. Sensing that there was still a better understanding to be had about Natalya, her caseworker lobbied strenuously within her agency to be allowed to seek a comprehensive psychological evaluation. The psychologist's report found Natalya to be a girl of above-average intelligence and suggested that it was highly likely that she suffered from fetal alcohol effect (FAE) as well as post-traumatic stress disorder (PTSD). The report went on to say that Natalya's traumatic history had left her feeling anxious and "on alert" much of the time. The FAE made it difficult for her to "hold on" to new learning. As a result, she often seemed to not know how to do things one day that she seemed to have mastered the day before. The psychologist recommended that the current foster parents take a Positive Discipline parenting class. The caseworker decided to attend along with them.

The particular Positive Discipline class the three of them took was called Positive Discipline for Children with Special Needs. When the class began, Natalya's foster parents, Galina and Ivan Marchenko, and her caseworker, Tamara, were merely hoping that they could learn a few new tricks to moderate Natalya's behavior. Natalya was doing poorly in school and had no real friends. Other children had learned to stay away from her because of her unpredictable aggressive outbursts. At home, Natalya presented herself as a somewhat sullen and self-contained little girl.

Galina and Ivan, themselves Russian immigrants, had successfully helped a great many struggling foster children, including several who had also come from Russia. They had also raised two children of their own who were off raising their own families. Natalya was quite a puzzle to them, and they were anxious to help her. During the course of the class, the foster parents learned many important new concepts, but three stood out for them. First, there was the basic Adlerian concept that all children want to belong and feel significant. They could look back on their years of parenting and foster parenting and see that they had understood this concept intuitively, even without having a name for it.

Second, they learned about the concept of "innocent behavior," that is, behavior that is driven by a child's special need and that isn't necessarily directed at anyone. They also learned (both on their own and with Tamara's help) about FAE and came to understand that a hallmark of children with this condition is that they sometimes do not seem to learn from experience. With this in mind, they began to see Natalya's struggles with belonging and social connection less as misbehavior and more as a set of skills that Natalya had simply not adequately learned yet.

> Innocent behavior is driven by a child's special need and isn't necessarily directed at anyone.

Third, they learned that an important aspect of developing a sense of belonging and significance is to give children the chance to make meaningful contributions. Frequently, in our culture we measure belonging by what benefits we derive from the group that we're in. Adler realized that giving back to the group and developing what he called *Gemeinschaftgefühl*, somewhat inadequately translated as "social interest," was at least as important.

> An important aspect of developing a sense of belonging and significance is to give children the chance to make meaningful contributions.

Bolstered by this new perspective, the Marchenkos decided not to take for granted that Natalya had the social skills that everyone had always assumed she had because she was so verbal and seemingly so intelligent. With help from Tamara, they looked at the steps involved in "simple" play interactions. An example was taking turns with a toy that more than one child wanted to play with. Galina and Ivan had assumed that Natalya, because of her previous experiences with deprivation, just didn't want to give up any toy she had because she believed that she would never get it back. When they, like previous adults in Natalya's life, insisted that she share toys, Natalya responded with adamant refusal, followed almost instantly by hitting or scratching. Even when they empathized with Natalya, indicating that they understood her reluctance to give up the toy, she still reacted aggressively. Their new understanding suggested to them that it was possible that Natalya could not "hold on" to the mechanics of trading toys back and forth. When she then refused (because at those moments she literally did not know how to do it), others reacted as if it were a willful decision. This reaction provoked the quick transformation of Natalya's innocent behavior ("I don't know how") into mistaken-goal behavior ("You can't make me!").

Ivan and Galina decided to *take the time to teach* Natalya the steps involved in sharing toys. Galina sat down with Natalya and the other two foster children in their home at that time (two girls ages five and nine) and showed them some pictures. In the first picture, a child is playing with a toy as a second child asks, "Can I have a turn?" In the second picture, the first child asks, "Can I have it back when you're done?" and the second child says, "Sure!" Finally, in the third picture, the first child gives the toy to the second child, who says, "Thanks!" (See figure 5.) Galina asked for the girls' help in cutting out the pictures and gluing them onto a piece of poster board. Then the four of them worked together to hang the poster board up in the playroom.

Galina explained that this is what happens when kids share toys. There usually was an opportunity to have another turn. She then acted out the scenario with two stuffed animals. Natalya did not immediately accept (or perhaps understand) that

Figure 5. Helping a child learn to share and take turns.

this applied to her as well. For the next several weeks, she still automatically said no when anyone asked for a turn with a toy she was playing with. However, instead of insisting that Natalya share the toy, Ivan and Galina showed her on the poster board how she could have another opportunity to play with the toy. Instances of aggression decreased almost immediately because no one was insisting that Natalya share the toys. Because her foster parents did not mistakenly interpret her refusal to share the toy as misbehavior, but instead saw it as innocent behavior, Natalya was not provoked to respond to a mistaken interpretation of her behavior and was freer to take in the learning of a new skill.

The Positive Discipline class also introduced Galina and Ivan to another tool that helped them both teach Natalya new skills and reinforce them. This tool was called Floortime and was originally developed by Dr. Stanley Greenspan as a way to enhance emotional interaction and understanding in children with special needs.[10] From a Positive Discipline perspective it also turned out to be a marvelous tool for getting into Natalya's world and building relationships with her. Using Floortime, Ivan or Galina would engage in pretend play with Natalya and follow along with whatever themes Natalya initiated. Initially their goal was simply to spend time with Natalya and help her see them as caring adults. They would follow Natalya's lead during their play with her and ended up playing out a number of elaborate themes, one of which revolved around stuffed animals refusing to share their toys and subsequently being punished for it.

> Floortime was originally developed by Dr. Stanley Greenspan as a way to enhance emotional interaction and understanding in children with special needs.

For Galina and Ivan it was an astonishing glimpse into Natalya's world. They saw how she had interpreted her early experiences of being deprived and punished and, more clearly, how previous attempts to "teach" her (whether by simple repetition, as at the McKenzies', or by punishing her, as in her previous foster homes) had left her both unskilled and confused. It was no wonder that she had reacted with such defensive intensity. In her view, she was continually being taken to task because she didn't have a particular skill. On one occasion, Ivan's stuffed animal got upset because he didn't want to share a toy. To his utter amazement, Natalya's stuffed animal drew him a chart just like the one Galina had drawn for the girls!

For a child with special needs, as you may recall, it is important to do two things. First, it is important that we acknowledge and accept the fact that the condition exists. As parents and teachers of these children, we must do our best to understand the condition itself and, even more crucial, the behaviors that might be associated with the condition. In Natalya's case, it was vital that the Marchenkos understand that her "failure" to display skills that she seemed to have already been taught was, in fact, a predictable by-product of fetal alcohol effect.

Second, it is critical that we not let the fact of the special condition block our vision of the child as a person with vast potential. The Marchenkos accepted the fact of Natalya's condition but not the idea that she could not learn. They simply (though in reality it was far from simple) rejected the use of punishment for teaching her and took the time to teach her in ways she could understand and even, in her play, teach others.

Natalya's progress in learning some new skills did not remake her overnight, as might be hoped for. She still was a girl for whom sullenness and aggression were frequently default positions. Other children did not warm up to her right away. In some ways, the Marchenkos' work had just begun. Now they needed to help Natalya feel connected to others and as if she had something to offer them in relationships.

POSITIVE DISCIPLINE TOOLS FOR BUILDING SOCIAL CONNECTIONS AND ENCOURAGING CONTRIBUTION

As your child with special needs grows, and especially as the difficulties associated with the condition become evident, it is easy to do the familial equivalent of circling the wagons—that is to say, putting up barriers between the family and the outside world. When the wagons are figuratively circled, it is easy for parents (and teachers) to imagine the world beyond the wagons as dangerous, callous, or (in the case of children whose public behaviors are challenging) simply too much trouble. It can start to feel easier and easier to limit contact with people who "won't understand."

This perspective, while completely understandable, does not move children toward the list of hopes and dreams we looked at in chapter 1. In fact, it creates a very real risk that our children will develop a sense of entitlement and will seek not to make connections but to put others at their service. To become the adults who have the gifts on that list, our children need frequent opportunities to feel reciprocally connected to other people and to make meaningful contributions to whatever groups they find themselves in. Adler called this "striving for superiority," by which he meant not to be better than others but to be the best we can be. Parents and teachers can help by using the following tools:

> To become the adults who have the gifts on that list of hopes and dreams, our children need frequent opportunities to feel reciprocally connected to other people and to make meaningful contributions to whatever groups they find themselves in.

- Structure experiences for your child that will foster this belief: "I am capable of warm relationships with others, and in these relationships I have something to offer."
- Focus on your child's strengths.
- Have faith and use encouragement to help your child do her best.

Structure experiences for your child that will foster this belief: "I am capable of warm relationships with others, and in these relationships I have something to offer."

It can be puzzling to decide how to help your child make social connections, especially when having trouble getting along with others has been a prominent feature of her life. Nevertheless, it is relationships that will be the vehicle for your child to grow, develop, and mature. The active ingredient in warm relationships is empathy; as Daniel Siegel put it, it is the experience of "feeling felt."[11]

As the Marchenkos learned more in their parenting class, they realized that to help Natalya strengthen her ability to develop meaningful relationships, they had to make sure that she felt understood and accepted by them. They continued their daily episodes of Floortime, during which they continued to follow Natalya's lead. In addition, they periodically introduced new wrinkles on old themes. For example, in one play session, Galina's stuffed animal started to cry, much to Natalya's surprise. Her first response was to ask Galina, not the animal, what the crying was about. In the voice of the animal, Galina bemoaned the fact that the animal did not know how to make friends and that no one liked her. Natalya quickly changed the direction of the play and, wisely, Galina followed along. Over time, she reintroduced similar wrinkles. On one occasion, Natalya seemed transfixed but did not change the theme. Galina whispered to Natalya in her own voice, "Do you have any advice for her?" Natalya said to the stuffed animal, "You should try playing games that the other animals like too." Galina's animal sniffed, "Thanks, I'll try that." In her pretend play Natalya was learning about the give-and-take that is so much a part of everyday relationships.

Focus on Your Child's Strengths

In planning experiences that will help your child develop both warm social connections and the ability to make meaningful contributions in those relationships, it is wise to build on the strengths that your child already has. In special education, there is the risk of overfocusing on children's deficits, trying to find ways to bolster children where they are weak. While helping children to improve areas of weakness is important, Positive Discipline, based on Adler's Individual Psychology, looks at children with special needs as whole human beings with both strengths and weaknesses and as having the potential to become contributing participants in a multitude of relationships.

As Natalya grew more comfortable and felt more accepted through her Floortime experiences, the Marchenkos, with the help and support of their caseworker and Natalya's therapist, began to think about how they could expand Natalya's range of positive experiences with relationships to include other children. For many parents of children with special needs, it can be a challenge to help their kids develop relationships with children their age, who can seem so much more capable. And unlike in Natalya's case, most of these children do not have to start building their relationship skills in their fifth family.

Galina had come to see Natalya's rich imagination and pretend-play skills as a great source of strength. She realized that this could be the foundation on which to help Natalya expand her relationship skills. Continuing her one-on-one Floortime experiences with Natalya, Galina asked her whether she would be interested in including Taneisha, Natalya's five-year-old foster sister, in some of their play. Predictably, Natalya was not keen on the idea until Galina explained that, first, she and Natalya would continue to have their own special time every day and, second, she could really use Natalya's play skills to help Taneisha learn to play better. (Taneisha also had come from an impoverished background and had been found to have some mild developmental delays.) Although still not completely sold, Natalya agreed.

At first, when the three of them played, Natalya had some trouble accepting that Taneisha might have different ideas about how the play might unfold. She was quick to react if she thought that Taneisha wanted something she had. Galina stayed patient and pointed out the sharing toys poster, reminding both girls that toys could be traded back and forth. Privately, Galina asked Natalya to think about ways Natalya might encourage Taneisha to play more creatively. She reminded her about the advice that Natalya's stuffed animal had given her own stuffed animal: to "try playing games that the other animals like too." Delighted that Galina had remembered this advice and seemed to think it was important, Natalya began to relish her role as mentor to Taneisha. On one memorable occasion, she started to become frustrated with Taneisha's somewhat inflexible behavior, looked at Galina, and said, "Oh, well. She's still learning."

Have Faith and Use Encouragement to
Help Your Child Do Her Best

Rudolf Dreikurs wrote that misbehaving children are discouraged children. What motivates them is encouragement. Both *discourage* and *encourage* come from the Latin root word *cor,* which means "heart." Children who are discouraged have lost heart and do not strongly feel that sense of belonging and significance. When we encourage children, we help their hearts to be strong. A very wise certified Positive Discipline associate in the Seattle area, Dr. Jody McVittie, says that "courage is the movement we make in the direction of becoming our best selves. Encouragement is the space we make for others to become their best selves—to exercise their courage."

As Natalya continued in her role as Taneisha's mentor, her ability to be a full play partner grew as well. On her best days, she could play for long periods of time with Taneisha, with and without Galina, during which time she shared both toys and decision making. Galina and Ivan now hoped to help Natalya apply these developing skills in her relationships with other children her own age. While Natalya's overall behavior at school had improved, she remained relatively isolated socially.

> Galina was acquainted with the mother of a little girl, Sophie, who was a classmate of Natalya. She called her, discussed her plan to expand Natalya's social horizons, and asked whether Sophie and she might be interested in meeting her and Natalya at the park. Sophie's mother agreed and they arranged to meet the next Saturday at the play structure in the park. Trying to keep expectations to a minimum, Galina shared with Natalya that they were going to meet Sophie and her mother at the park for a playdate.

> Natalya's reaction was, as Galina might have predicted, reserved. As Saturday grew closer, Natalya seemed to grow more nervous and short tempered. On Thursday evening at bedtime, she burst into tears when she couldn't find a favorite stuffed animal to sleep with. With Natalya curled up in her lap, Galina asked her whether she might be worried about playing with Sophie at the park. Natalya nodded and the two of them sat quietly for several minutes. Finally Natalya said, "Sophie doesn't like me. None of the kids like me." Galina reflected back that she could see that Natalya was worried that no one liked her. "I bet that makes you feel pretty lonely at school." She then asked

what kinds of games Sophie played at recess. Natalya described the pretend games that she had seen Sophie and the other kids playing. Galina nodded and said, "Hmm. I know someone else who is always pretending to be a superhero princess too." Natalya sat quietly. Galina went on, "I have played lots of pretend games with you, and I know how much fun we have. You are a girl who has great ideas for playing. I really have faith that you and Sophie will have fun together, even if you are nervous right now. I can't wait to hear about it."

In her conversation with Natalya, Galina took Natalya's concerns very seriously. With her *empathetic statement* she conveyed to Natalya that she understood Natalya's feelings of isolation and loneliness. Then she made an observation about Natalya's play skills that only someone who had spent hours playing with Natalya could have made. She ended with a statement of faith in Natalya's ability.

On the actual playdate with Sophie, Natalya was clearly very nervous and did not engage in pretend play with her usual abandon. Galina and Sophie's mom watched the play from a distance while sitting and chatting on a park bench. On the way home, Natalya said that the play was "sort of fun." Galina told her that she knew how hard it could be to do something you were really nervous about. "But you know what?" she added. "Even though you were nervous, you did it, and it looked like you had at least a little fun. Shall we meet Sophie at the park again?"

"No," Natalya said. "Can she come over to play?"

POSITIVE DISCIPLINE TOOLS RELATED TO YOUR CHILD'S MISTAKEN GOALS

Even while Natalya's social skills were noticeably improving, things did not always go smoothly. As Ivan and Galina discovered, not all of the behaviors they saw in Natalya were "innocent." There were times when the Mistaken Goal Chart proved invaluable to them. While Natalya's relationship with both of her foster parents was growing closer, it seemed to them that there were still times when they found themselves feeling angry and challenged by her behavior. After first looking for the possibility that this was innocent behavior, they came to the conclusion that it was more likely that Natalya was pursuing a sense of belonging through the mistaken goal of misguided power. An example was her frequent refusal to do household chores that had been assigned to her, such as setting the table for dinner. Frequently, she would procrastinate while watching television, agreeing to set the table but simply not doing it. This was especially difficult for Ivan. With him, Natalya's passive refusal soon turned into a shouting match between them that resulted in Natalya losing privileges, such as a later bedtime than Taneisha's.

When your child with special needs is engaging in behaviors that leave you feeling angry, challenged, or defeated, consult the Mistaken Goal Chart. It provides several tools that will help her gain a sense of belonging and significance in ways that promote both your relationship with her and a feeling of contribution to the family. Among the tools are the following.

Let Routines Be the Boss

Well- and jointly planned routines can take the place of many a struggle between parent and child. A routine, especially one that the child has helped create and that is posted, makes it much more difficult for your child to prolong the struggle with you. After all, it is not just you telling your child to set the table; it is the posted and agreed-upon routine doing so.

Remembering how successful Galina's poster about sharing and trading toys had been with Natalya, Ivan waited until the next family meeting and asked for help in designing a routine for afternoons after school. With considerable input from the three girls, an agreement was worked out. It spelled out all of the things that needed to happen between coming home from school and bedtime. It included both tasks that needed to be done (like setting the table) and fun activity options (like television or playtime). The girls agreed that they would rotate the tasks periodically so that no one got stuck with something she didn't like for too long. Again with help from the girls, the routine schedule was drawn onto poster board and hung in the playroom. (For Natalya, Ivan asked if there were any tasks for which she thought additional, step-by-step pictures might be helpful.)

Be Kind and Firm at the Same Time

As we have said elsewhere in this book, being both kind and firm at the same time is a crucial Positive Discipline skill. In our culture in general, we often like for things to be one thing or the other, black or white. We imagine that things are easier with this kind of simplicity. However, when we take the time to examine an issue, it often turns out to be one thing *and* the other. Such is the case with kindness and firmness. Excessive reliance on kindness leads to our parenting or teaching permissively. Excessive reliance on firmness leads to our parenting or teaching rigidly. It is by doing both *at the same time* that we parent or teach authoritatively, or from a Positive Discipline perspective.

Even with the routine chart, Natalya was not always willing to perform her chosen task. When she refused by either procrastination or belligerence, Ivan responded with both kindness and firmness. If Natalya was watching a television show, he would ask her what the routine chart indicated that it was time to do (letting the routine be the boss). If Natalya started either procrastinating or arguing, Ivan would make an empathetic statement like "I can see that you're really enjoying this show." (Being kind.) He would follow it by standing in front of the television, smiling and pointing to the dining room, where the table was waiting to be set. (Being firm.)

It should be noted that it is often true that children, either with special needs or otherwise, don't necessarily dwell on the *kind* part of the message. None of us remembers any of our own children or the children we have worked with saying to us (either verbally or nonverbally), "Thanks for delivering that unwanted message about setting the table so kindly." While we have not given up hope completely that our children are, in the long run, appreciative of our kind and caring style, we take solace in the fact that children tend to cooperate much more when we are both kind and firm at the same time. In addition, we are encouraged that new research by Jody McVittie and Al Best has been published that supports our conviction that children's social-emotional development can greatly improve in the context of relationships with adults whose parenting or teaching styles are both benevolently responsive and respectfully demanding, that is, kind and firm at the same time.[12]

Offer Limited Choices

Children who are pursuing the mistaken goal of misguided power still need power, as do we all. It is the sense that they must have inordinate amounts of power to feel belonging and significance that we must help them with. It is easy for us as parents and teachers to "get hooked" when children demand unreasonable amounts of power and to react by seizing all of the power ourselves. ("I'm the adult here! You will just do what I tell you.") Instead, we must keep in mind that seeking some level of power is simply part of being human. We can help them by offering limited and developmentally appropriate choices.

When Natalya continued her quest for misguided power, it was very helpful for either Galina or Ivan to remember the concept of limited choices. Thus, even when she balked at letting the routine be the boss about setting the table, Ivan could get through to her by asking something like, "Which do you want to put down first, plates or cups?" Another way he found to offer choices was to put pictures of the table items in a big hat and let Natalya choose the order that way.

Ask for Help

It is remarkable how frequently children become more cooperative when we ask for their help instead of telling them what they must do. It is an apt illustration of how forward thinking Adler was in noting how important making a contribution is to the sense of belonging.

> It is remarkable how frequently children become more cooperative when we ask for their help instead of telling them what they must do.

In the mornings, Natalya (and, truth be told, her foster sisters too) tended to dawdle. They had a routine chart for the morning as well, and it was pretty clear that they all knew what to do. But to Galina's chagrin, the girls all moved as if they were walking through molasses. On mornings when she had to be out the door at a certain time to get the girls to school and make scheduled appointments, she sometimes reverted to "drill sergeant mode." Not surprisingly, the girls did not find this motivating.

One day, the morning after one of her Positive Discipline classes, she sat down with the girls and said, "Girls, I really need your help this morning. I need to make sure that I get to my appointment on time. What can you do to help me out?" The girls quickly decided on what tasks they could do and did them. It wasn't until later that Galina noticed that these were the same tasks that they had picked for that week's routine chart.

Use Family Meetings

Family meetings are a Positive Discipline tool that helps children learn many skills essential for living in a democratic society. They communicate the importance of each family member's contribution and, in doing so, reinforce the sense of belonging within the family. It is not uncommon for families who have children with special needs to underestimate the importance of the sense of belonging, especially if their child's condition makes communication difficult. It is also easy for these families, equally unintentionally, to underestimate the ability of their child to make meaningful contributions.

As described above, the Marchenkos used family meetings in order to encourage Natalya to make a contribution toward improving the family's daily routine after school. In doing so they were also helping Natalya find more socially useful ways to be powerful.

Among the other skills that can be learned through family meetings are the following:

- Problem solving
- Future planning
- The ability to wait
- The ability to take turns
- Managing feelings of frustration and disappointment
- Understanding someone else's viewpoint

POSITIVE DISCIPLINE TOOLS PRESENTED IN THIS CHAPTER

1. Take the time to teach.
2. Engage your child through Floortime. (The corresponding Positive Discipline tool is "Get into your child's world.")
3. Structure experiences to help your child develop a sense of connection and capability.
4. Focus on your child's strengths.
5. Have faith and use encouragement to help your child do her best.
6. Use empathy.
7. Let routines be the boss.
8. Be kind and firm at the same time.
9. Offer limited choices.
10. Ask for help.
11. Use family meetings.

DAMON'S STORY:
FOCUS ON YOUR CHILD,
NOT ON THE LABEL

Five-year-old Damon is being raised by his great-grandmother. In an era when family bonds seem to be increasingly fraying, Damon's situation is not uncommon. Damon's mother was developmentally disabled and, more than likely, retarded (intellectually disabled). She gave birth to Damon while still living at home and soon moved across the country to live with a man she met on the Internet. Damon's grandmother was in poor health and asked her mother, Damon's great-grandmother, to help out. As the grandmother's health continued to deteriorate, his great-grandmother's "helping out" eventually meant adopting Damon and taking responsibility for raising him. His mother has not seen him in well over two years.

Damon's great-grandmother, Barbara, became involved in his life soon after his birth. It was she who noticed that his development seemed to be lagging. When he was first assessed by a local early intervention program at eight months of age, Damon did not qualify for services. It was suggested to the family, however, that he be rereferred closer to his third birthday if they continued to have concerns.

By the time he was two years and ten months old, Damon's developmental difficulties were more obvious. Instead of talking, he was still pointing and making gestures when he wanted something. Simple tasks seemed quite hard for him. He could not stack blocks. Even though it kept frustrating him, he continued to put smaller blocks on the bottom and larger ones on top. Taking off his clothing, even simple things like sweatpants, proved enormously complex for him. He could not use utensils to feed himself and was very easily frustrated.

Barbara was remarkably patient with him, showing him again and again how to do the things that seemed beyond him. She reported, "It just breaks my heart when he starts crying because he can't do something simple." Barbara got in the habit of anticipating his needs and doing things for him so that he wouldn't get so frustrated.

When Damon was three years old, two important events occurred. First, his mother, Darla, returned to the area and wanted to see him. She marveled at how cute he was but didn't understand why he couldn't get himself dressed or use the toilet on his own. One weekend, Barbara took a well-deserved break and left Damon in the care of Darla and her mother, Damon's grandmother. During this weekend, Darla decided that Damon should be potty trained. She brought him to the toilet and told him she would give him candy if he peed in the toilet. Damon got very excited when he heard the word candy but did not use the toilet. When several attempts to entice him in that way were unsuccessful, Darla grew frustrated and angry. She brought him to the toilet and told him he had to sit there until he peed in it. Damon did not understand and grew quite fearful in response to Darla's insistence that he stay on the toilet. He tried to get up and run away, but Darla held him down. After this occurred several times, Darla's mother intervened and demanded that she stop. At this point Damon was terrified of even approaching the bathroom.

The second major event for Damon was that he was reevaluated and this time qualified for early childhood special education. The only area of development in which Damon seemed close to other kids his age was gross motor skills. His development in cognitive (thinking) skills, expressive and receptive language skills, fine motor skills, and daily living skills (like dressing or feeding himself) was significantly delayed in comparison to other children his age. The program did not use a test to assess Damon's intelligence; however, it was speculated that he would likely fall within the higher range of mental retardation (intellectual disability).

At this point, Darla returned to her life across the country and Damon was enrolled in a developmental-skills group offered by the early childhood special education program. At first this experience was very positive for Damon. He loved being around the other children, an experience he was not used to, as he lived in a rural area. His ability to communicate grew as he started to put together three- and four-word phrases and sentences. He was able to let his teachers know, to some extent, what he did and did not want and to make simple choices between two offerings.

At the same time, relatively simple things like taking his coat off or putting it in his cubby continued to be very difficult for Damon. One of the first phrases he began to use consistently at school was "You do it." Seemingly whenever a request was *made of Damon to try something, he would respond with that phrase: "You do it." His teacher's attempts to break tasks down into smaller steps were met with tears and a staunch refusal on Damon's part followed by "No, you do it!"*

Damon's play in the group grew rougher. While it did not seem as though he was actually trying to hurt anyone, Damon's relatively well-developed skills in running, jumping, and climbing, coupled with his seeming lack of ability to understand the consequences of how he played, led to several children getting hurt. In frustration, Damon's teacher, Cathy, resorted to giving him punitive time-outs when he hurt someone. He would always look remorseful, but the behavior continued.

In addition, Cathy grew frustrated because she perceived that Barbara was "pampering" Damon at home by not putting limits on his gross motor play. She also felt that her attempts to help Damon become more independent (by learning to put his coat on or by using the toilet by himself) were being undermined by Barbara's insistence that Damon was still traumatized by the thought of using the toilet and by her tendency to step in too quickly and do things for him.

For her part, Barbara believed that Damon was simply being punished in class (by being given time-outs). She told the teacher that Damon was only being told what not to do but not taught what to do instead. She believed that the teacher did not help Damon enough and that it was cruel, given his obvious limitations, to let him struggle with tasks that were beyond his ability level. Finally, she pointed out that Damon was beginning to resist going to school and saying that he didn't like it.

By mutual agreement, a consultant skilled in Positive Discipline was asked to observe Damon, talk to both Barbara and Cathy, and determine whether she could help the two of them work together in Damon's best interests. One of the first things she suggested was that both Barbara and Cathy take the Positive Discipline for Children with Special Needs class to gain an understanding of the basic philosophy behind the skills they would be learning.

When Barbara heard at Damon's evaluation that it was likely that he was mentally retarded, she made certain assumptions about his capabilities. After all, she had been the first one to see how his development had lagged. The label "mentally retarded" only confirmed what Barbara had both believed and feared about Damon's limitations. She felt justified in her beliefs that Damon should be spared frustration and that he needed the kind of help that some would label pampering.

In both special education and medicine, labels are used to classify children (and adults) with impairments. Ideally, a label gives a "ballpark" in which parents and teachers can begin to better understand their children's needs. The ballpark is meant to define a generality. Thus, when we say that a child has mental retardation, there is a set of characteristics that will be common among children with that condition.

Within the ballpark it is our responsibility to understand each of our children as an individual; all children with mental retardation do not look or behave alike. Just like other children, these children will be interpreting their life experiences and making decisions about what they must do to belong and feel significant. The tools they have at their disposal to do this will be different, and perhaps more limited, but the process will happen nonetheless.

> Within the "ballpark" it is our responsibility to understand each of our children as an individual; all children with mental retardation do not look or behave alike. Just like other children, these children will be interpreting their life experiences and making decisions about what they must do to belong and feel significant.

Over the course of the last generation or two, our culture has undergone a sea change in terms of the way special needs are understood. Gone are the days when children with special needs could be excluded from schools or child-care centers. While it has not been completely eradicated, the stigma associated with many different conditions has been greatly reduced. But even without stigma, what remains is insidious.

What happens when we confuse the ballpark with the child within it?

One outcome is what former president George W. Bush once called "the soft bias of low expectations." In hearing that Damon was mentally retarded, Barbara flashed immediately to the ballpark of what that label would likely mean for Damon. In doing so, she accepted the *fact* of Damon's condition but she also let this *fact* block her vision of his *potential*.

Taking the Positive Discipline for Children with Special Needs class together proved to be an enriching experience for both Barbara and Cathy, Damon's teacher. Each of them realized that they had been coming at the issue of helping Damon from opposite directions. When Barbara learned about the concept of "innocent behavior," her first thought was that she had been right all along to give Damon the amount of "help" he seemed to need. After all, it was his likely retardation that was making it so difficult for him to learn. When Cathy learned about the concept of "mistaken goals," she at first thought that she had been right to hold Damon responsible for his behavior. Over the course of the class, however, they each realized that they were both right and that they each needed the perspective of the other to do their best for Damon.

Especially after the potty-training incident, Barbara was sensitive to how easily Damon became overwhelmed and frustrated by his lack of understanding. It seemed natural to her that he needed to be treated extra kindly in order to feel better about himself. Plus, it really did break her heart when she saw him struggling and miserable.

In the class, Barbara learned about the concept of *kindness and firmness at the same time.* When she began to understand that excessive kindness at the expense of firmness led to pampering, she could see that it wasn't always helpful to avoid situations where Damon had to struggle to achieve something. She was able to understand that some struggle helps children develop their "capability muscles."

> Struggle helps children develop their "capability muscles."

Working together with Cathy and Damon, she created a visual system that illustrated the process of putting on various articles of clothing. She also *took the time to actively teach* Damon each step individually. The difference in her orientation this time was that she now believed in his capacity to learn, even if at a slower rate.

One day, when Barbara came to school to pick Damon up after class, she pointed to his coat when he started to walk out the door without it. She said, "Damon, get your coat on first." Quite agreeable, Damon went to his cubby, got his coat, made one unsuccessful attempt to get it on, and handed it to Barbara, saying, "You do it." Catching the teacher's eye, Barbara pointed to the first picture (hanging on Damon's cubby) and asked, "What do you do first?" (This was a wonderful example of the use of *curiosity questions* to help children learn to become problem solvers.) Damon looked at the picture and put his left arm through the sleeve. Barbara said, "You did it! What comes next?" Damon made two quick attempts to get his right arm in the sleeve and then started to cry. "You do it! You do it!" Barbara used an *empathetic statement,* saying, "It's frustrating that your arm won't go in that sleeve!" and followed it up with an *encouraging statement,* "I'll wait right here with you while you keep trying. I know you can do it." This sequence needed to be repeated twice more, but then Damon got his own right arm through the sleeve. Instantly, his face lit up and he shouted, "I did it!"

POSITIVE DISCIPLINE TOOLS TO FOCUS ON YOUR CHILD, NOT ON THE LABEL

Damon was a lucky boy, although he was unaware of that fact. He was fortunate because his great-grandmother, Barbara, had learned a supremely important lesson. She had learned that the ballpark, i.e., mental retardation, did not completely define Damon. Yes, it suggested that there would be limits and accommodations that would apply to and be necessary for him. But it did not mean that he could not learn or that he could not belong and feel significant. Garry Landreth, an award-winning play therapy teacher and mentor to many, has a wonderful phrase that encapsulates the need to see past children's impairments. In *Play Therapy: The Art of the Relationship,* he reminds us: "Focus on the donut, not on the hole."[13]

The following will help parents and teachers focus on the donut:

- Assist other family members, service providers, and colleagues in reversing their own low expectations for your children or students.
- Take care of yourself.

Assist Others in Reversing Their Own Low Expectations for Your Children

Parents of children with special needs and, to a lesser extent, these children's teachers, have a double burden in this regard. As we saw with Barbara, it can be difficult and may take a while for parents to both accept the *fact* of their children's condition and maintain the ability to see their children's *potential*. Having done so, however, their job is not done. It is likely that others who will play important roles in their children's lives will need help to view them holistically and not simply through the lens of their disability. Parents will need to be the advocates for their children's right to struggle. (This is not to say that they will not need to advocate for logical accommodations for their children as well.)

> Parents will need to be the advocates for their children's right to struggle.

In both families and classrooms, it is often an unspoken goal that things go smoothly so that the learning plans for the whole class can proceed without undue interruption or so the family can get out the door quickly. This is not an unworthy goal. Because we teach children in group settings and because the family *group* has legitimate needs, there is some urgency that the children learn in the context of the group (the class or family), even when some children might be struggling. In any group setting, even in self-contained special education classrooms, where the law reminds us to be aware of each child's Individualized Education Plan, there is a constant tension between the needs of the group as a whole and the needs of the individual children who make up the group.

Because this is true, a tendency can arise, despite the best intentions of everyone involved, to do more for children with special needs than is good for them, so that the experience of the group they are in (the family or the class) can proceed smoothly. Think of a caterpillar in a chrysalis. It is the struggle to emerge that strengthens the muscles that become the wings of the butterfly. Without the struggle, the butterfly's potential will go unrealized. Again, let us stress that we are not advocating leaving children with special needs without the support they need. There must be a balance that both accommodates their special needs and encourages them to reach.

Because the toileting incident with Damon's mother, Darla, had affected him so dramatically, Barbara was reluctant to leave Damon with anyone. After a while, however, she did meet a young mother who also lived in her rural community. She had a son who was Damon's age and went to the same community preschool as Damon. The two women struck up a friendship and began to go to each other's houses to chat and let the boys play together. Barbara noticed that Damon frequently grabbed toys after he watched his new friend play with them; it seemed that he wanted to try to do what he had just seen. The boy, not surprisingly, did not like this much and would yell at Damon to give him his toy back. At first, the boy's mother tried to get him to play with a different toy, saying, "It's okay. Damon doesn't know how to share yet. Just let him play with it, okay?"

> Think of a caterpillar in a chrysalis. It is the struggle to emerge that strengthens the muscles that become the wings of the butterfly. Without the struggle, the butterfly's potential will go unrealized.

Barbara caught a glimpse of the future there and saw people, with the kindest of intentions, making allowances for Damon. (We should note here that *allowances* are not the same as *accommodations*. Allowances tend to constitute pampering and actually inhibit learning. Accommodations are systems put into place to help a child with special needs learn skills that may come more easily to other children; they level the playing field so that learning can take place.) She saw how limiting this would be for him. It reinforced what she had been learning in her class. She thanked the young mother for her kind intentions and said, "I've been learning how to help Damon ask for turns." From her purse she took out a ring

Figure 6. Portable Problem-Solving Pictures.

with several small laminated pictures attached. (See figure 6.) One of them showed a child asking another child for a turn. Getting Damon's attention, she showed him the card. His eyes flashed with recognition and he said, "I want a turn."

Take Care of Yourself

On a commercial airline, at the beginning of any flight, the flight attendant goes through a set of safety instructions. One of them has to do with a sudden drop in cabin pressure. If there is such a drop, we are told, oxygen masks will automatically drop down. We are then instructed to put our own masks on first before we try to help our children put theirs on. The implication is that we will be unable to help our children if we don't take care of ourselves first.

This is excellent parenting advice as well. For many parents, however, it goes against the grain; we are used to putting our children's needs first and foremost. It is easy for parents to become so consumed with all of the tasks of raising children that they can find their own inner resources dwindling. The flight attendant's admonitions are very appropriate here; if parents are unable to meet their own basic needs, they will be ill equipped to meet their children's. It is at times like these that we find that our "lids flip" most easily.

For parents of children with special needs, this is even truer. As we have seen, the number of balls in the air that need to be juggled can be overwhelming. Couple that with the guilt that often overlies everything, and things can become critical. So how can you take care of yourself?

In our classes we devote time to helping parents answer these questions for themselves. We have discovered that the question of how to take care of yourself is actually two questions: How do you take care of yourself in the moment when your child is

> We are used to putting our children's needs first and foremost. It is easy for parents to become so consumed with all of the tasks of raising children that they can find their own inner resources dwindling. The flight attendant's admonitions are very appropriate here; if parents are unable to meet their own basic needs, they will be ill equipped to meet their children's. It is at times like these that we find that our "lids flip" most easily.

screaming at you and you are about to be overwhelmed by the stress? And how do you take care of yourself over time so that those kinds of stressful moments happen less frequently? It is sometimes helpful to think of it as you would car maintenance. When things break down on the road, you have to do something immediately to get moving again. On the other hand, regular maintenance makes breakdowns on the road less likely.

Over the years, parents and teachers in our classes have made lists of things they can do in the moment when they feel that they are about to be overwhelmed. The lists typically include but aren't limited to the following:

- Breathe. Deep breathing has actually been found to reduce the level of cortisol, the stress hormone, in our brains. In fact, if you stand with your hands clasped behind your back, your body will automatically be in the right position to do "belly breathing."

- Walk away, even if just for a moment or two. Brain research tells us clearly that the heat of the moment is not the time when we do our best problem solving. At that point, our brains are in "fight or flight" mode. By walking away, we will also be modeling for our children how to calm down.

- Use humor and/or do the unexpected. Once, Damon was screaming at Barbara that he wanted her to build him a block structure, which she thought he could do for himself. Empathetic statements weren't helping and she couldn't walk away because he just kept following her. She grabbed an old cowbell that she kept on a shelf and rang it, shouting, "And that's the end of this round, ladies and gentlemen! Be sure to stay tuned to see Damon try to build the tower one more time!" Damon burst out laughing and said, "You silly, Grandma."

- Count to ten slowly. This is a longstanding remedy that has taken on the status of an old wives' tale. However, it can be very effective in helping you get to a place where you can make a decision more calmly.

- Trade off, if that's an option for you. Sometimes, a different person's handling the situation changes the dynamic just enough to bring some calm. One couple shared that they agreed in advance that the other could step in when one of them "lost it." Since they had agreed in advance, when one of them stepped in (so the one who had lost it could take a break), it was accepted with gratitude instead of defensiveness.

- Self-talk. Remind yourself of things that you have learned. For example, Barbara frequently reminded herself that struggling was not a bad thing for Damon. She found that this helped her resist giving in to his piteous crying.

Parents have made similar lists of ways that they can take care of themselves over time. These lists typically include but aren't limited to the following:

- Exercise. Take walks. Ride a bike. Do anything that gets you moving.

- Work in the garden.

- Read. Reading in and of itself can be relaxing. In addition, several parents have mentioned joining book groups as a way to both read and have time around other adults.

- Listen to music.

- Join a support group. There are active support groups for just about every special need.

- Spend time with friends.

- Spend nonparenting time with your partner.

- Especially if you are a single parent, find someone you can trust to watch your children so that you can get breaks. This can be extended family or friends. In some communities there is a service called respite care available through public or nonprofit agencies. (Budget cuts on every level have made this service harder to find.)

The items on the second list above take planning and commitment. Greg Crosby, a professional counselor and trainer in Portland, Oregon, teaches us something that should come as no surprise to anyone: Pleasurable activities, the kind of activities that can build up your emotional reserves, do not happen without a plan. All of us have said things to ourselves like, "I really should get out and walk more." Barbara found that, for her, the key was in making a specific plan. "On Saturday, Annie will watch Damon for me for three hours. I'm going to take the dogs for a long walk in the woods."

> Pleasurable activities, the kind of activities that can build up your emotional reserves, do not happen without a plan.

POSITIVE DISCIPLINE TOOLS RELATED TO YOUR CHILD'S MISTAKEN GOAL

As Barbara was changing the way she understood what was helpful to Damon at home, his teacher, Cathy, was undergoing a similar process with Damon in the developmental-skills group. While she had been right about Barbara's tendency to pamper Damon at home, she began to see that her more punitive responses to Damon, born of her frustration, had not been helpful either.

One of the more pleasant outcomes of Barbara and Cathy's attending the Positive Discipline class together was their growing ability to pool their resources and work together without feeling as though the other one was wrong. As a result, they were able to help each other see that one result of Damon's having been pampered for so long was he had grown quite accustomed both to the inordinate amount of adult attention he had received and to adults doing things for him when he was upset.

In particular, Cathy noted that she frequently had felt annoyed or irritated by Damon's behavior, as well as occasionally worried (and guilty) that perhaps she had not helped him enough when he seemed to be struggling. The first question she asked herself was whether the behaviors that she saw in Damon were "innocent," i.e., simply the result of his significant cognitive limitations. To help her answer her question she reflected on how Damon had reacted with Barbara that time when he had not wanted to put on his coat. She and Barbara had both worked diligently to create a visual system for Damon and to effectively teach him all of the steps. Furthermore, she had seen him use the pictures many times to remember the steps. She concluded that when Damon now whined about performing a similar task and demanded that Cathy do it for him, her feelings pointed to his mistaken goal and not to innocent behavior.

A glance at the Mistaken Goal Chart showed that Cathy's feelings (annoyance, irritation, worry, and guilt) suggested that Damon's mistaken goal was undue attention, and even more specifically special service, a particular kind of undue attention. That being the case, Damon's belief was "I count or belong only when I'm being noticed or getting special service. I'm important only when I'm keeping you busy with me." (Of course, this belief behind Damon's behavior was outside his awareness.)

When your child or student with special needs is engaging in behaviors that you have determined are not an artifact of his condition and are leaving you feeling as Cathy was, consider some of the following tools.

Allow Disappointment and Frustration as New Skills Are Developed

If you think back to any time you have learned a new skill, chances are that the process did not go smoothly. Most skills take a while to learn and even longer to master. Along the way, we frequently become frustrated or disappointed that we are not mastering the skill as fast as we might like to. *These feelings are a part of the process.* We can almost never achieve independence or competence without them. Alfred Adler would say that our drive to overcome these feelings of "inferiority" is part of what makes us human and creates a drive for improvement.

When Damon first started in the developmental-skills group, he clearly did not know how to ask for

> Most skills take a while to learn and even longer to master. Along the way, we frequently become frustrated or disappointed that we are not mastering the skill as fast as we might like to. *These feelings are a part of the process.*

turns with toys or equipment. In addition, he had grown used to being given what he wanted. Cathy created visual systems that illustrated how to ask for turns. She also gave him frequent verbal cues (e.g., "Damon, remember to ask if you can have a turn"). Initially, what tended to happen before Cathy could prevent it was that Damon would grab or push first and ask the question later. The two of them would then look at the visual schedule and practice how to ask for a turn. Frequently, however, especially if Damon had just hit or pushed the other child, that child would say no when asked for a turn. Cathy then made an empathetic statement about Damon's disappointment, but she did not change the outcome.

Teach Problem-Solving Skills

When children are engaging in behaviors designed to keep us involved with them or to get us to do things for them, it is frequently because they do not have the confidence to solve a problem on their own. Seeking undue attention or special service keeps them from stretching to learn tasks that seem too difficult.

Early on at school, as illustrated above, Damon began to develop a reputation with the other children. He had bowled them over or grabbed things from them frequently enough that even when he began to master the skill of asking for toys or equipment first, other children still frequently refused. At that point Cathy began to teach Damon the "art of negotiation." When another child said no to Damon, Cathy taught him to ask, "When can I have a turn?" (The whole class was learning this process as well.) Cathy would then help both children arrive at a number of minutes and ask if they wanted to set a timer so that they would know when the one's turn was over.

We should stress here that an understanding of numbers or time is not necessarily important in this process. (Cathy related a story about when, after asking how many minutes until his turn, Damon was told, "Two." True to the spirit of a born negotiator, he argued, "No, three.") The skill being taught here is give and take. If there is an understanding of numbers, that's just icing on the cake.

Provide Special Time

An important thing to keep in mind about undue attention is that it's the "undue" aspect that is problematic; all children need attention. Providing special playtime that is regular and guaranteed is a way to help children learn to fill other time by entertaining themselves.

Part of what Damon had learned in his young life was that he was *entitled* to Barbara's attention pretty much whenever he wanted it. He also believed that, even when he had Barbara's full attention, it was her responsibility to do for him all of the things he did not believe he could do for himself. This, of course, was a draining responsibility for Barbara. As a result of taking the Positive Discipline class, she realized how all of this undue attention was holding Damon back. She began by having several short "special times" a day with Damon on the days when he did not go to school. During those times she focused on playing what Damon wanted to play.

In the meantime, Barbara made a choice board with things that she knew Damon really liked to play and that she was confident he could play without her. The list included pictures representing cars, blocks, dinosaurs, and a few other favorites.

At first, while Damon loved special time, he did not quite understand why all time could not be like that. He did not like it when a special-time episode ended. Barbara empathized with his disappointment and also stuck to her plan. She told Damon she was really looking forward to their next special time and was now going to do a household task or read a magazine. She showed him his choice board and encouraged him to choose one of those activities.

Initially this was not a smooth process, but Barbara persevered, neither arguing with Damon nor giving in to him. She allowed him to have his feelings and had faith that he could work through them. Over time Damon discovered that he could indeed occupy himself and have fun.

Provide Opportunities to Make Contributions

When any child, with or without a special need, is pursuing undue attention, it is helpful to turn the tables. Instead of being drawn in and reacting to feelings of annoyance or irritation, redirect your child or student by asking him to perform a meaningful job. This will allow him to gain attention in socially useful ways.

In the classroom, Damon frequently got overstimulated in gross motor play and, in his exuberance, bowled smaller children over. Rather than continuing to focus her attention on behavior that she had spoken about with Damon repeatedly, Cathy instead put her arm around his shoulders and asked him to come with her to help put out play-dough toys. This had the double advantage of redirecting Damon away from the overexuberant play and allowing him to make a contribution to the whole group. Now there was a new, fun activity for everyone to do, one that Cathy knew was a favorite of Damon's as well.

Use Encouragement

When children who are seeking either undue attention or special service are learning new ways to get socially useful attention or to function more autonomously, it is helpful to make encouraging statements instead of giving praise. Encouragement, among many other advantages, communicates to children that they are noticed and appreciated and that what they do matters. Praise frequently rewards a finished product, while encouragement emphasizes effort and contribution. (See the appendix, the Praise vs. Encouragement Chart.)

Both Barbara and Cathy became masters at providing Damon with encouragement. At home, Barbara told him things like, "I really appreciated your help setting the table tonight. It made my job much easier." At school, Cathy made a point of providing encouragement, especially when Damon persisted with a frustrating task. Once, when Damon really wanted a turn with a red tricycle, his classmate refused to answer his "how many minutes" question. Damon followed him around and kept repeating, "You have to say two or three minutes!" Cathy gave him a big hug and said, "You are *really* trying to get Collin to answer you!"

Damon grew in his capabilities and his self-confidence. Barbara and Cathy did as well. Neither of them became perfect (none of us do), but they both began to learn from their mistakes and to focus on the child and not the label.

POSITIVE DISCIPLINE TOOLS PRESENTED IN THIS CHAPTER

1. Be kind and firm at the same time.
2. Take the time to teach.
3. Ask curiosity questions.
4. Use empathy.
5. Encourage.
6. Assist others in reversing their low expectations of your child.
7. Take care of yourself.
8. Allow disappointment and frustration as new skills are developed.
9. Teach problem-solving skills.
10. Provide special time.
11. Provide opportunities to make contributions.

LANCE'S STORY: INSPIRE YOUR CHILD THROUGH YOUR INTERACTIONS

Five-year-old Lance had been diagnosed at a very young age with a significant hearing loss. A comprehensive evaluation by his local early childhood special education team when he was three years old determined that, in addition to his hearing impairment, Lance demonstrated delays in important developmental skill areas: communication, social/emotional functioning, and daily living skills. Lance's eligibility for early childhood special education services, combined with an unsuccessful community preschool experience, led his parents and educational team to place him in a highly supported early childhood special education preschool setting for his year preceding kindergarten.

In the first few weeks in his new school setting, Lance clearly preferred to play by himself during the free-choice play activities, both inside the classroom and outdoors. He adamantly refused to participate in all other activities: circle time (which included songs and stories), snack, art, and game time. Lance used nonverbal communications to signal his refusal of activities offered. He would turn away and not attend to the person making the offer or simply move away from the person. Occasionally he would push the person away. Attempts to guide Lance using a gentle hand-hold when moving from one place to another in the classroom or outside the classroom would usually result in one or all of the following: a physical struggle, a flop to the floor or ground, screaming, and darting away.

Lance's multidisciplinary educational team had a combined wealth of experience teaching children with significant communication and behavior challenges. Even with all of their training in the techniques of behavior management prominent in the field of special education, as well as in the endorsed methods of teaching young children with hearing loss and developmental delays, the team struggled. During the early weeks of his placement, Lance's team could find no strategy effective in motivating him to participate in any activities other than his preferences. What made teaching Lance new and needed skills even more challenging for his team was that, even while they were engaging with him in activities he chose, he usually did not accept a direction or suggestion (through any mode of communication: verbal, sign, or picture symbol). On those rare occasions when he began to participate in a shared activity with his instructor, he not only stopped the engagement when his instructor gave him positive feedback for his involvement in the activity but would often actively disengage (push away the toys that were part of the interaction, turn his body to one side, and move away).

Lance's team respectfully considered the impact of his hearing *impairment on his delayed communication and social skills. However, through Lance's repeated refusals to interact with them in any kind of shared engagement, even in an activity of high interest, it became clear to his instructors that he was clearly and emphatically deciding not to be taught by any of them. His team's challenge that school year was not merely in changing Lance's behaviors, i.e., replacing the many ways that he resisted with behaviors of engagement and coopera-tion. Their greater challenge was to comprehend and help him change the beliefs that led to the decisions he was making about how to behave. Lance's teacher had recently completed a work-shop in Positive Discipline and decided to look through the lens of this approach to understand Lance and consider ways to help him make choices that would increase his openness to learning from others.*

In Positive Discipline, we acknowledge the potential limitations that a particular handicapping condition has on a child as well as the cor-responding learning challenges that the child may face. However, our greater focus is on how to inspire children with special needs to view themselves as connected, capable, caring, and contributing members of their families and their communities, despite their impairment(s). As much as we encourage parents and educators to use Positive Discipline tools to help change children's misguided behaviors into more respon-sible and socially acceptable ones, the foundation of our efforts is to teach parents and educators the tools that help children make decisions to engage in socially useful ways, which ultimately will lead to a genuine sense of belonging and significance.

> The foundation of our efforts is to teach parents and educators the tools that help children make decisions to engage in socially useful ways that, ultimately, will lead to a genuine sense of belonging and significance.

In Lance's case, motivating him to make decisions that would lead him to increased learning in a social context was no small task. His methods of disen-gagement were worrisome to his teachers, especially when he became aggressive toward others. Lance's team decided to try the Positive Discipline approach, which his teacher believed could be valuable both in understanding his resistance to social engagement and in helping him welcome relationships with others as a meaningful context for learning.

Lance's team was challenged to "think outside the box" of the approaches they had learned over the many years of their combined training, due to Lance's negative response to these approaches. For example, he was quick to pick up on any efforts of the staff to "manipulate the contingencies" (the things that preceded or followed his behavior), and he would find ways to circumvent the positive behavioral contingencies ("rewards") set up to entice him. He also did not respond when the team tried different ways to help him take in auditory and visual information.

Lance's team came to see that Positive Discipline offered them two important lessons for responding to the challenges they faced with Lance. First, it offered them an opportunity to focus on their own behaviors related to their *style* of interacting with children like Lance. Specifically, they learned about an ***authoritative style of engagement.*** This style of interaction is neither authoritarian nor permissive. It is mutually respectful, encourages cooperation from the child, and supports the child's ability to learn self-management (in contrast to adults' "managing" the child). Lance's instructors learned that the behaviors associated with an authoritative style of engagement were exactly the behaviors that they wanted to elicit from Lance. Lance's teachers wondered: If Lance could observe and experience the respect and encouragement that comes from an authoritative style of teaching, would his openness to engaging with and learning from his teachers increase?

Second, Positive Discipline offered the staff on Lance's team a framework that looks beneath the surface of a child's behavior, past the antecedents and consequences that are apparent on the observable surface, to the mistaken beliefs that underlie the behaviors. Based on what they hypothesized was Lance's mistaken goal, the team was able to consider a variety of Positive Discipline proactive and encouraging responses designed to boost his sense of belonging and significance as he interacted with and learned from others.

When you are perplexed by your child's behaviors that get in the way of his ability to build relationships with others and to learn skills that strengthen his sense of capability, consider (1) Positive Discipline tools that will help you sustain an authoritative style of engagement with your child even when he is refusing to learn from you, and (2) your child's mistaken goal and the related Positive Discipline tools you can use to help your child increase his sense belonging and significance through positive connections with others and increased competence.

POSITIVE DISCIPLINE TOOLS THAT INSPIRE YOUR CHILD THROUGH YOUR INTERACTIONS

Your child learns a great deal from how you interact with him, even if his actions make it seem otherwise. If your parenting or teaching style is authoritative (by which we mean kind and firm at the same time, as well as mutually respectful), you will increase the likelihood that your child's social development will be enhanced. While children with more typical patterns of development have fewer obstacles to learning from their experiences than do children with cognitive, communication, social, and/or sensory impairments, your child with special needs will nevertheless learn from your authoritative style of engagement as you use these Positive Discipline tools:

> If your parenting or teaching style is authoritative (by which we mean kind and firm at the same time, as well as mutually respectful), you will increase the likelihood that your child's social development will be enhanced.

- Model the interactions you want for your child.
- Focus on winning children over, not winning over children.
- Exercise kindness and firmness at the same time.
- Provide encouragement to your child.

- Build on your child's strengths.
- Implement respectful forms of limit setting.

Model the Interactions You Want for Your Child

How will your child learn to show respect for others, to communicate and listen, to demonstrate patience, to share, to cooperate and negotiate, to problem-solve with flexibility, to empathize, and to demonstrate concern and compassion for others if you are not modeling these during the many interactions that you have with your child each day? We believe that even the most impaired children learn and grow from positive modeling by others. If you want your child to become more flexible in problem solving, show him how flexibility "feels" through your own demonstrations of flexibility as you engage with him. If you want your child to cooperate more, cooperate with him.

Modeling the interactions you want to see manifest in your child may not be the only tool you use to teach the important skills listed above, but it certainly is a place to start, especially with children who show a strong resistance to learning from you. Again, we don't mean to imply that this is an easy road. It can be difficult, for example, to stay cooperative and flexible in the face of your child's inflexibility and refusal to cooperate.

> If you want your child to become more flexible in problem solving, show him how flexibility "feels" through your own demonstrations of flexibility as you engage with him. If you want your child to cooperate more, cooperate with him.

Probably highest on the list of behaviors that Lance's instructors needed to model with Lance was patience. In the early weeks of his placement in the ECSE setting, when he needed considerable one-on-one support, Lance's active opposition to staff requests and to the group's agenda was so frequent that members of his classroom team requested that no one of them be exclusively assigned to him. His instructors realized that approximately every hour, a "break" from Lance was needed, as the longer they spent with him, the more depleted their patience would become.

In addition to patience, Lance's instructors interacted with him displaying many of the desirable social behaviors they wanted to see him develop. They showed interest in and attention to him by watching him as he played and by giving him eye contact and smiles when he looked at them. They spoke to him in a kind tone of voice even while increasing their voice volume due to his hearing loss. They shared toys that they were holding while playing with him, and they negotiated with him if they wanted a toy that he was holding. Their body movements were visible and predictable to him, and they avoided any physical interaction with him that he might misinterpret as force. They demonstrated empathy when he was sad or upset, and they offered comfort in the form of hugs whenever he accepted these. It was their hope that, at the very least, modeling positive behaviors for him would *not* invite negative behaviors. Further, by modeling positive behaviors, there was a chance that he would feel and experience what these behaviors could be like for him and begin to view positive actions as the model for his own behavior.

Focus on Winning Children Over, Not Winning Over Children

One of the risks you may face as a parent or teacher of a child with special needs is the inclination to do things for your child that he or she can learn to do independently or with partial autonomy. Similarly, when your child behaves in ways that are not socially useful, you may feel inclined to immediately take charge by "making" him stop or "making" her behave differently. You may do this even though, ultimately, you look forward to the time when your child, without your assistance, will stop the misguided behavior and act responsibly. In order to help your child gain greater skill in managing his or her own behavior, we suggest that you avoid trying to control your child and instead focus on winning cooperation.

Positive Discipline's *Four Steps for Winning Cooperation* are (1) expressing an understanding of your child's feelings; (2) showing empathy for your child's point of view, which doesn't mean that you agree with it; (3) sharing your feelings and perceptions when your child is ready to listen; and (4) inviting your child to focus on a solution. With Lance, these steps were presented very simply due to his developmental delays, his communication impairment, and his limited social interest. Also, it should be noted that verbal information was presented to Lance with increased volume due to his hearing impairment. Visual information was presented simultaneously with words in the form of pictures and Signed English that highlighted the concepts of the verbal messages. The following is an example of how the Four Steps for Winning Cooperation were used with Lance.

FOUR STEPS FOR WINNING COOPERATION

1. Expressing an understanding of your child's feelings

2. Showing empathy for your child's point of view (without necessarily agreeing with it)

3. Sharing your feelings and perceptions when your child is ready to listen

4. Inviting your child to focus on a solution

When playing outside during recess, Lance was always given a five-minute warning before recess ended. At the end of the five-minute period, his teacher showed him the "snack" picture and said and signed, "It's time to go back to school for snack time." If Lance began to scream and move away from his teacher, she usually would say and sign something like, "Lance, you are sad. You don't like to stop playing outside."

While her understanding and empathy elicited Lance's momentary attention, he didn't usually stay around long enough to listen to much more. Lance's teacher, persistent in her effort to gain Lance's cooperation in the transition back to school, usually shared a perception like "You brought snack today. You like snack." She would continue to run alongside him on the playground (as he ran away from her), saying and signing, "Do you want to run back to the school or walk?" offering him limited choices as a solution. He, of course, continued running, and she turned the fleeing/pursuing activity into the "I'm gonna get you!" game. Lance usually began giggling and looking back to watch his teacher chasing him. She positioned her moving body in relation to his moving body in such a way that he often raced back into the classroom, exactly where the snack activity was happening!

It is clear by this example that cooperation is not an all-or-nothing condition. Instead, it is a quality that is "to a greater or lesser extent." In Lance's case, his movement into the classroom occurred to a large degree as a function of having fun engaging in a chase game and to a lesser degree because he was cooperating. In this early stage of winning Lance's cooperation, his teacher *avoided taking control over* Lance's movement. She *didn't force him* to follow through on her communications, as physically guiding him to carry out the desired behavior would only lead to physical resistance and struggle and not to true cooperation. Instead, she enticed him to cooperate of his own volition.

As you read the above example, you may have been thinking that Lance's teacher was, in fact, "giving in" to him by interacting with him positively after he had "refused" to comply with a request. In response, we will just remind you of Positive Discipline's long-term perspective. His teacher was not interested *simply* in gaining Lance's compliance. In the context of positive, respectful interactions with him, she wanted to help him learn to think flexibly, to consider the point of view of others, and to develop self-management.

Exercise Kindness and Firmness at the Same Time

Learning to set reasonable and safe limits for your child while maintaining a kind, even-tempered disposition is an important authoritative tool of Positive Discipline. Your ability to be gentle and steadfast *simultaneously* at critical junctures with your child (for example, when your child is extremely upset and engaging in screaming, temper tantrums, self-injury, and/or aggression) will enable you to learn how it *physically feels* to express kindness and firmness *at the same time*. This style of interaction is not a midpoint between being kind and being firm. Instead, through your body's serene, even-paced movements, your calm, neutral tone and volume of voice, and your persistent, unswerving stance, you respectfully communicate and follow through on an expectation that you have for your child.

> Learning to set reasonable and safe limits for your child while maintaining a kind, even-tempered disposition is an important authoritative tool of Positive Discipline.

An example of this occurred with Lance when it was time for recess. He was quick to run to the outside door of the classroom when he was told that it was time to play outside. Due to the staff-to-student ratio in his classroom, it was safest for Lance and his classmates if all eight of them left together with the four or five adults who were teaching that day. Often arriving first at the doorway, Lance was inclined to push the door open and run to the playground unaccompanied. His teacher, anticipating his actions, usually blocked the doorway and held the door closed until all were assembled to leave as a group. When Lance tried to push at her to get to the doorway, she was prepared with pictures combined with her signs and words, communicating "stand at door" and "wait for friends." Her body language was not abrupt or harsh; instead it was predictable and composed. She partially squatted, meeting him at eye level. And her voice was pleasant and upbeat. Yet she did not budge from her position of guarding the doorway, because it was her ultimate goal to guard against any harm that could come to Lance if he left the classroom without the company of an adult.

Provide Encouragement to Your Child

Your child will be inspired to behave in socially useful ways if your statements are encouraging and supportive and respectfully recognize her constructive actions as well as her responsibility in initiating these actions. Your encouraging remarks should call attention to your child's actions, focusing on her specific efforts and accomplishments. Provide encouragement soon after the deed, and use language that is understandable to your child. Augment your spoken words with sign language and/or pictures as needed. Enhance your communication with eye contact and with affirming facial expressions and tone of voice. Especially for younger children, who often shout "Look at me! Look at me!" words of encouragement convey the message that we are indeed looking at them and that what they do is important.

> Your child will be inspired to behave in socially useful ways if your statements are encouraging and supportive and respectfully recognize her constructive actions as well as her responsibility in initiating these actions.

The encouragement that was provided to Lance was simplified to match his ability to understand language. The encouraging comments were made with both increased volume and augmentation (signs and pictures) due to Lance's hearing loss. Lance's teachers made a great effort to communicate with him at his eye level so that he could see and understand their facial expressions. When Lance began, in small ways, to demonstrate social interest and cooperation with others, his instructors offered encouragement such as "You came to circle!" "You are painting!" "Thank you for waiting!" Lance did not reject the encouragement that his instructors provided, likely because it focused on what *he* did and not what *they* wanted him to do.

Build on Your Child's Strengths

Highlighting your child's strengths and helping him use them to improve areas of weakness will have multiple benefits for your child. In doing this, you will assist him in focusing attention on constructive actions. Engaging in constructive actions, and experiencing the good feelings that result from these, will increase his sense of significance and capability. Further, by maintaining your attention on your child's strengths, you will be more likely to interact with him in a confirming, optimistic way; this, in turn, will enhance your relationship with him. Hence, focusing on your child's strengths will lead him to increased feelings of competence and connection that will ultimately improve his ability to behave in socially useful ways.

> Focusing on your child's strengths will lead him to increased feelings of competence and connection that will ultimately improve his ability to behave in socially useful ways.

Consider what activities your child with special needs is good at and is motivated to engage in. Provide opportunities for him to build on these strengths. Consider activities that allow him to use his strong abilities to improve his areas of weakness. In Lance's case, his gross motor abilities were on par with those of other children his age, and he greatly enjoyed engaging in activities that involved running, jumping, and climbing.

When his teacher set up plastic bowling pins in the classroom one day and modeled for the students how to use a bowling ball to knock the pins over, Lance decided to disregard the bowling ball and to jump over the pins instead. His teacher, seizing this as a possible opportunity to increase interaction with Lance, followed his lead by also jumping over the bowling pins. Lance responded with smiles as he watched his teacher, and then repeated his actions. His teacher repeated, and Lance again followed, clearly delighted to have a play partner with whom to hurdle over the bowling pins. In this situation, an activity that involved Lance's strong motor ability was used to strengthen his social engagement and reciprocal turn-taking skills.

Implement Respectful Forms of Limit Setting

All children, including children with special needs, need to be kept safe from harm. Further, they need to learn how to respectfully interact with others and how to show consideration for the living and nonliving things they encounter. One of the ways to help your child stay safe and accomplish the skills she needs to learn is through your use of Positive Discipline guidelines for limit setting. These are the same for your child with special needs as the guidelines for limit setting for all children.

> For children who are developmentally young, *supervision, distraction,* and *redirection* are critical tools for ensuring your child's safety and for showing your child what she can do instead of what she can't do.

A central Positive Discipline guideline for limit setting is one we addressed above: Demonstrate firmness accompanied by kindness. Another important guideline is to involve children when setting and enforcing limits. You can respectfully do this by generating solutions together instead of "managing" the child. However, if your child is developmentally younger than four years old, even if he is chronologically older, you will need to take responsibility for establishing the limits and following through, remembering to do so with kindness and firmness at the same time. For children who are developmentally young, **supervision, distraction,** and **redirection** are critical tools for ensuring your child's safety and for showing your child what she can do instead of what she can't do.

It is never helpful to use punitive treatment as a method of limit setting with your child. While punitive methods may seem to work (as they usually do stop behaviors in the short term), they are not useful (in the long term) for the development of the skills and traits on your list of hopes and dreams for your child. If your child behaves in ways that cause harm to others, to herself, or to property, it's possible that she needs a break from the situation at hand until she calms down significantly enough to engage in problem solving. A positive time-out area (that your child has helped design) might be a welcome place where she can recover from significant states of agitation. (See chapter 4.) Included in the positive time-out area might be items that help your child to self-soothe and feel better. Items that calm your child, as well as visual displays (with photos, pictures, and/or words) that encourage your child to think about useful behaviors, can be available in the positive time-out area.

If your child becomes even more upset when moving, or when it is suggested that he move, to the positive time-out area, it's best to remain calm and create the experience of positive time-out exactly where he is. Items that you know elicit more composure in your child can be offered. You might model taking exaggerated deep breaths or hand your child a favorite stuffed animal. You might merely sit close by while your child works through her feelings. When your child is calm enough to reestablish a connection with you, follow the Four Steps for Winning Cooperation as described above. Augment your spoken words with sign language and/or pictures (that are already prepared or that you draw on paper or a whiteboard).

Overall, if your limit setting leads your child to feel more connected and competent, you will have positively supported your child. For Lance, limit setting was needed during the early months of his placement in the early childhood special education preschool, when he had not yet learned to respect others while he was in a high state of emotional arousal. During his episodes of significant emotional upset, displayed through temper outbursts and acts of aggression, Lance often welcomed the option of a positive time-out area, especially when his teacher accompanied him. Over time and as his connection with his teacher became stronger, Lance became more competent in self-managing when he became upset.

THE POSITIVE DISCIPLINE TOOLS RELATED TO YOUR CHILD'S MISTAKEN GOAL

During his first few weeks of placement in the early childhood special education preschool setting, Lance's team felt challenged by the misguided behaviors he displayed in the form of refusals to join class activities. His instructors soon discovered that when they offered him even the slightest amount of assistance in joining an activity, he reacted by intensifying his challenging behaviors. Given the teachers' own emotional reactions, i.e., feeling challenged and defeated by Lance, the belief behind his behaviors appeared to consistently arise from the mistaken goal of misguided power. His *misguided* behaviors seemed to come from his mistaken belief that he belonged and was significant only when he was in control and when no one else was telling him what to do or what not to do.

If your child is acting out of the mistaken goal of misguided power, you can use proactive and encouraging responses to help him discover how he can feel a positive, satisfying, and developmentally appropriate sense of control while contributing to his family and community. Those tools that were helpful with Lance in addition to the tools we highlighted earlier in this chapter are described below.

Avoid Power Struggles

It takes more than one person to engage in a power struggle. If your child's behavior challenges you, avoid getting pulled into a conflict. Instead, withdraw from the potential struggle. If it's safe for your child and others, you can withdraw physically by walking away and then returning a short time later, when your child is calm, to reintroduce whatever it was that provoked your child in the first place. Keep in mind the "brain in the palm of your hand." (See chapter 3.) Neither your child nor you can do effective problem solving with a "flipped lid."

> Neither your child nor you can do effective problem solving with a "flipped lid."

If your child's safety or that of others is at risk if you walk away, you can withdraw from potential struggle by staying physically present, allowing your emotional state to become neutral (taking deep breaths might help), and waiting patiently until your child is calm before you present the earlier situation again. Either response will allow you the time needed to consider whether or not to modify the situation when you re-present it to your child. Lance's instructor responded to his behavior by staying physically present and maintaining a neutral disposition. Not only did this response keep Lance from escalating the behavior of concern, but it also gave his instructor time to evaluate whether the original situation that had triggered Lance's upset needed to be presented differently in order to make it more understandable and tolerable for him.

We understand that becoming neutral and waiting patiently are often easier said than done. There will be times when you do not meet this high standard. This will happen not because you are weak but because you are human. Remember: Mistakes are opportunities to learn.

Don't Fight and Don't Give In

Withdrawing from a power struggle with your child doesn't mean that you are withdrawing from the opportunity to teach important skills. If what you tried to do was reasonable but still led to resistance, you may need to try again after your child is calm. If you decide to change your interaction somewhat, you will still need to do so after your child is in a calm state. In either case, you might anticipate that your child will refuse again to go along with your idea. Should this occur, withdraw again from a potential power struggle and wait for her to become calm. Remain kind and firm and emotionally calm as you reintroduce the expectation.

> Remain kind and firm and emotionally calm as you reintroduce the expectation.

Whenever Lance's or his classmates' safety was at risk, Lance's teacher remained steadfast in her efforts to prevent injury from occurring. Lance, who was more inclined to run through the small classroom instead of walking, sometimes accidentally bumped one of his classmates, causing the student to lose balance and occasionally to fall. Lance's teacher reasonably required that Lance walk through the classroom. She used the picture of "walk" to augment her words, she provided a gentle touch on his chest to slow down forward movement, and she provided encouraging comments whenever he did walk. If he began to physically resist her attempts to help him slow down, she held firm to her expectation in a benevolent way. If her firmness provoked him to respond with greater resistance and to have a tantrum, then she would wait patiently for him to calm while maintaining her expectation that he walk in the classroom.

Provide Opportunities for Your Child to Use Power Constructively

When your child is acting out of the mistaken goal of misguided power, his underlying belief is that a sense of belonging and significance will be achieved if he is in control and no one is in charge of him. Your child's *struggle* to maintain control will never satisfy his striving for belonging and significance because fighting with others leads to unstable relationships, which, in turn, put the sense of belonging and significance at risk.

To counterbalance your child's struggle to maintain control, provide opportunities for your child to use his power in helpful ways. For example, because Lance was interested in and competent at activities on the preschool playground, his teacher often brought some of his classmates to play next to him so they could learn a gross motor or independent-play skill by imitating him. Also, whenever it was possible and reasonable for Lance to take the lead in a situation within his preschool setting, his teacher allowed him to "take charge." Through a variety of situations in which Lance was given an opportunity to be a leader, his teacher hoped to replace his misguided attempts to achieve power with more socially beneficial actions.

> To counterbalance your child's *struggle* to maintain control, provide opportunities for your child to use his power in helpful ways.

Offer Limited Choices

Everybody likes having options in life, and your child is no exception. Helping her recognize that she does have options will increase her sense of control over her life. Provide choices to your child in a clearly understandable format, such as spoken words, pictures, or object representations. Present a reasonable number of choices depending on the situation and your child's understanding: as few as two; probably no more than sixteen if you are using the Wheel of Choice. (See figure 7.)

Offer choices when your child is in a calm state, as decision making and other problem-solving skills are less likely to be utilized when she is in a state of high emotional arousal. Remember that the choices you provide should take into consideration the needs of your child, your own needs, and the needs of the situation.

Figure 7. Wheel of Choice.

Sometimes your child may need a break from a demanding situation or to delay her response to an expectation. If it's reasonable for the situation, make sure that your choices include an option to take a break and an option to wait. Providing these options won't remove the expectation. It will simply delay it until you can revisit it at a later time when your child is in a more receptive state. Combining this tool with other Positive Discipline tools will increase the likelihood that your child will become more receptive to reasonable expectations. If your child who is acting from the mistaken goal of misguided power experiences her power to choose socially useful options in accordance with her own time frame, she will be more likely to view these choices as her own.

> Offer choices when your child is in a calm state, as decision making and other problem-solving skills are less likely to be utilized when she is in a high state of emotional arousal.

Lance's teacher provided many opportunities for Lance to make choices throughout his preschool day. Given his hearing impairment and delayed communication skills, pictures on a choice board, as well as simple drawings of his options on a whiteboard, were presented to him. Because the concepts of a "break" and "wait" were not totally understood by him, his teacher watched his body language and physical actions. These signaled his interest in ending something or stopping an action. She began teaching him to sign "all done" when his actions communicated the desire to end an activity. He himself spontaneously began to put his outstretched arm in front of his chest, with flat palm facing the adult, to signal "stop." By acknowledging his hand gestures, "all done" and "stop," and by offering him visually presented options, his teacher hoped to increase his sense of control over his life.

Practice Follow-Through

Effective follow-through involves four steps: (1) In a constructive conversation with your child, invite him to share his feelings and thoughts about the situation; (2) Use brainstorming with your child to generate possible solutions, and choose one that you mutually agree on; (3) Decide together a specific time deadline; and (4) Follow through in a kind and firm way if your child doesn't keep the agreement.

EFFECTIVE FOLLOW-THROUGH

1. Invite your child to share his feelings and thoughts about the situation.

2. Use brainstorming to generate possible solutions; choose one that you both agree on.

3. Decide together a specific time deadline.

4. Follow through in a kind and firm way if your child doesn't keep the agreement.

Given Lance's hearing impairment and communication delay, the steps of follow-through needed to be modified. Initially, Lance's teacher did the talking/signing because he didn't speak/sign to her. She shared what she noticed about his feelings and what he might be thinking about the situation. For example, if he began to show signs of upset when it was announced to the class that it was time to put away toys and get ready for snack time, his teacher would say and sign to him, "You are sad. Play time is all done." She would also show him pictures on a Velcro strip (e.g., pictures representing "sad," "play," "all done") in order to increase his understanding of her communication to him.

Lance's teacher further modified the follow-through steps because Lance was not yet able to brainstorm solutions, nor was he able to understand time concepts. Instead she offered him limited choices. For example, she asked while pointing, "Do you want to put away *this* toy or *that* toy?" If Lance made a choice about which one to put away but didn't begin the cleanup process, she would follow through by reminding him: "You chose to put away _____." She often *pointed* to the toy, without talking, in order to follow through with kindness and firmness. When Lance eventually started putting away the toy he had chosen, his teacher expressed appreciation (saying and signing "Thank you!") and encouragement ("You are putting away the _____").

Spend Special Time with Your Child

Sharing pleasant experiences with your child will strengthen your relationship as well as increase opportunities for you to provide encouragement. Lance's teacher joined him in play frequently during his preschool day. Initially, she would simply sit on the floor near him and observe him. Then she began to play parallel to him using the same kinds of toys that he used. Eventually, she started employing humorous or silly play with her toys to get his attention. If he showed interest in her play, she offered him a turn, trying to remain nonthreatening. Her goal was to share special time with Lance so that he would remember his time at this special preschool as being filled with enjoyable times more than with struggles.

REVIEW OF POSITIVE DISCIPLINE TOOLS PRESENTED IN THIS CHAPTER

1. Model the interactions you want for your child.
2. Focus on winning children over, not winning over children.
3. Exercise kindness and firmness at the same time.
4. Provide encouragement to your child.
5. Build on your child's strengths.
6. Implement respectful forms of limit setting.

7. Provide supervision, distraction, and redirection.
8. Avoid power struggles.
9. Don't fight and don't give in.
10. Provide opportunities for your child to use power constructively.
11. Offer limited choices.
12. Practice follow-through.
13. Spend special time with your child.

ARI'S STORY:
BELIEVE IN YOUR CHILD—
THE SELF-FULFILLING PROPHECY

A spongy child-size football flew onto the floor near the front passenger seat, accompanied by a piercing, raspy scream. Hurled with great force by three-year-old Ari, the ball just missed the side of Ilana's head. Eight-year-old Ilana, seated in the passenger seat, continued reading her book, only momentarily taking her eyes off the page to notice the speeding object in her peripheral vision. "Ouch! Stop pulling my hair! Mommy, Ari is hurting me!" yelled five-year-old Dalia, who was sitting next to her little brother in the backseat. In a strained tone of voice, Mara, mother of the three, slowly answered, "Just give him one of his toys to hold, Dalia." In her usual style, Mara tried to maintain composure as she drove her children through heavy city traffic after picking up her girls from school. Dalia's face registered surprise and then immediately exploded into tears. As Dalia pushed Ari's hands away from her head, she demanded, "Stop!" Ari, in turn, matched her volume with a loud bellow and pushed back. The ruckus in the backseat continued for the next five minutes until Mara pulled into their driveway.

Ari, who always accompanied Mara and his sisters on these weekday trips, was usually a congenial traveler as long as he could hold and play with a favorite toy while riding in his car seat. Occasionally, however, a noise from another vehicle or racket from construction work on the street irritated him. He often responded to these sounds by shrieking. Sometimes he intensified his expressions of irritation by also throwing toys, kicking at the seat back in front of him, and grabbing things within reach, including Dalia's toys and hair.

Mara was usually quite resourceful when responding to Ari's irritable moments. After all, she had gained considerable understanding of Ari since his birth, not only because she was an attentive and loving parent but also because she had spent a great deal of time learning about Ari from the standpoint of his doctors, his vision specialists, and his early intervention team. At birth, Ari had shown signs of severe vision impairment; although he was able to respond to some visual input, he was considered legally blind by medical standards. In addition, he showed significant delays in motor and communication skills during his first year of life. Given his vision impairment and developmental delays, Ari qualified at a very young age for early intervention services in his school district's early childhood program.

Mara had absorbed all the advice and tips that Ari's therapists and specialists had shared with her, and she had diligently followed through with whatever therapeutic activities they had recommended. She was able to keep Ari calm and content in the car when they were alone together. However, when Ari's sisters were also in the car, Mara was often stumped about how to handle Ari's upsets, especially when they involved his run-ins with Dalia.

Mara felt ambivalent as she responded to the clashes that arose too frequently between her two youngest children. On one hand, she felt very sad about Ari's limitations and worried about his future potential. She wanted his precocious sisters to treat him with tolerance and compassion. On the other hand, while she felt disappointed with Dalia's lack of patience with Ari, she also felt guilty about having such high expectations of her five-year-old daughter. Mara recognized that for the past three years of her young life, Dalia had been required to make room for a little brother who arrived in this world needing a great deal of time, attention, and energy from his parents. Also, while Mara and her husband, David, tried to consciously and equitably respond to the needs of each of their children, they were quite aware of how much Ari's activities consumed their waking hours. Whereas Ilana, their older daughter, was resilient, self-directed, and generally easygoing about the attention paid to Ari by her parents, Dalia was often inflexible, clingy, and moody when she had to share one or both parents' time with Ari.

As Mara pulled into the driveway, relieved that she and her children had arrived home safely, she realized that the relationship between Ari and Dalia needed to change. She committed herself to figuring out how her three-year-old with significant handicaps and her talented five-year-old could learn to get along better. It was true that attending to Ari's unique and demanding developmental needs had to be a priority for her and David. Yet it was equally true that their family's long-term health depended on helping their children live together peacefully.

While focusing intently on the many details of daily caregiving and supportive activities for your child with special needs, it can be difficult to refocus the lens in order to look at the bigger picture and imagine your child in the years ahead. Yet in order to help your child move forward to a more optimistic and promising future, it is important to envision valuable characteristics and life skills for your child. These characteristics and life skills form significant landmarks toward which you can direct your energy and attention. With this vision of your child's future in mind, believe in his ability to make progress toward these landmarks. Your use of Positive Discipline tools to empower your child to develop these important skills will assist you to take steps as if the results are attainable. The steps you take will help you and your child make progress on your journey together as he develops desirable characteristics and life skills.

Mara's challenging car ride ended with her recognition of the need for an improved relationship between Ari and Dalia, as well as with hope for long-term harmony within her family. Positive Discipline offers many tools that can help parents like Mara and teachers of children with special needs to believe in their children's ability to develop important characteristics and life skills, and to assist their children in making progress toward these long-term aspirations.

POSITIVE DISCIPLINE TOOLS TO HELP YOUR CHILD DEVELOP THE VALUABLE CHARACTERISTICS AND LIFE SKILLS YOU ENVISION

When you believe that your child will develop the characteristics and life skills that you anticipate for him, you activate the *self-fulfilling prophecy*. This is the principle that suggests that our beliefs about our children's ability to be successful will influence both our interactions with our children and their own belief in their ability to be successful. This, in turn, leads to progress toward the goal. Essentially, if we hold on to beliefs about our children's ability to make progress toward long-term goals, there is an increased likelihood that what we predict will become true.

Focusing on the characteristics and life skills that you envision for your child with special needs can be a very powerful exercise. By using Positive Discipline tools to help your child progress toward these long-term goals, you will benefit from the optimistic and constructive outlook that accompanies this endeavor. Such an outlook will affirm your efforts when your path with your child is smooth and will keep you afloat when the journey with your child is rough. Think about the following Positive Discipline tools to help you achieve a long-term view of your child:

> Essentially, if we hold on to beliefs about our children's ability to make progress toward long-term goals, there is an increased likelihood that what we predict will become true.

- Identify your hopes and dreams for your child.
- Empower your child by . . .
  - Avoiding pampering.
  - Putting kids in the same boat:
    - Provide accommodations for your child with special needs.
    - Listen to all your children.
    - Give all your children consideration and empathy.
    - Offer your children opportunities to find resolutions to their conflicts.
    - Use communication adaptations with your child with special needs if these are needed.
  - Taking time for teaching.
  - Focusing on small steps.
  - Providing encouragement.
  - Showing faith in your child through your energetic support.
  - Letting go and taking care of yourself.

Identify Your Hopes and Dreams for Your Child

In chapter 1, you had the opportunity to engage in an exercise that parents and teachers in our groups participate in during their first Positive Discipline class. You imagined a visit from your child thirty years from now. You listed qualities that you would like to be true about this adult in the future. These characteristics and life skills form a *list of hopes and dreams* that you have for your child. Now find this list if you developed it while reading chapter 1, or generate a list right now. As you review your list, consider the following questions to assist you in helping your child make progress toward these long-term outcomes: What can *you* do to help your child reach this potential? As you think about your child's network of support, who can assist you in your efforts?

Both your attitude and your actions will influence how successful you can be in maximizing your child's potential. It is important to realize that the characteristics and life skills are a long-term view of your child, and while he may not demonstrate these qualities now, he can learn to develop them over time, or at least move in that direction. When considering discipline methods, remember that the root word for *discipline* has to do with teaching; refer to this list often and ask yourself, "Does this discipline method help my child develop these characteristics and life skills?" It can be highly motivating to affirm in your mind that these qualities are attainable and proceed as if they are possible. Set your intention for your child to eventually attain these qualities.

> It is important to realize that the characteristics and life skills are a long-term view of your child, and while he may not demonstrate these qualities now, he can learn to develop them over time, or at least move in that direction.

You may want to keep your list of hopes and dreams for your child with you or post it in a prominent place where you can be reminded of them regularly. If you are a parent or teacher, you can use your list as a guide when you participate in your child's school team to develop educational goals for him. As a parent, you can use the list as you seek therapeutic services for your child or when you hunt for recreational activities for him. Periodically review the list to gain perspective on your child's progress toward these significant goals and to gain new insights about ways to accelerate movement toward your hopes and dreams for your child.

As you think about all those who can help you on your journey with your child, consider the following exercise. On a sheet of paper, draw a small circle in the middle of the page. Next, draw a series of concentric circles around the small circle. In the center of the small circle, write your child's name. In each of the concentric circles, starting with the one nearest to your child's name, write the names of people in your child's life, from those who are closest to him and who know him very well (in the inner circles) to those people in your child's life who are less well acquainted with him (in the outer ones). (See figure 8.)

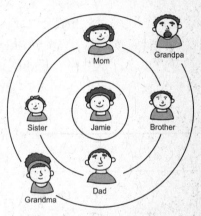

Figure 8. Network of Support.

When you have added the names of all the people connected to your child, you have developed a simple representation of your child's **network of support.** In the spirit of the African proverb "It takes a village to raise a child," it can be said, "It takes a network of kind, caring, and accommodating individuals to fuel the ongoing movement of a child with special needs toward a promising future." Your child's network will also become *your* important supportive connections as you help your child to become the person you believe him capable of becoming.

If you have developed the circles-of-support diagram as a parent, the closest people to your child are you and your immediate family. If you have developed it as a teacher, the closest people to your child are you, his classmates, and his other educational team members. These individuals, who spend the most time with your child, are key players in his social network. Engage them in supportive roles to assist you as you help your child build skills today that will eventually lead to his future accomplishments. For example, Mara's focus on improving the relationship between

> It takes a network of kind, caring, and accommodating individuals to fuel the ongoing movement of a child with special needs toward a promising future.

Ari and Dalia will be a major step toward fulfilling Mara's dream for Ari: long-term harmony for him within his family. Because Dalia is a key player in Ari's life, Mara can caringly involve Dalia in helping to solve the challenges of peaceful car travel.

The most important actions you can take to propel you and your child toward the realization of the characteristics and life skills you want for him is to regularly employ the following Positive Discipline tools.

Avoid Pampering

Alfred Adler used the concept *Gemeinschaftsgefühl* to describe one of our highest callings as human beings: achieving a sense of community and actively working to contribute to this community.[14] *Gemeinschaftsgefühl* is the condition of feeling genuinely connected to others and sincerely concerned about the welfare of others. We act on this sense of connectedness and concern for others by actively taking responsibility for contributing to the well-being of our community.

The characteristics and life skills that we envision for our children often reflect the traits that we value most in human beings, including qualities associated with *Gemeinschaftsgefühl*. When we asked the parents and teachers of children with special needs from our Positive Discipline classes to identify characteristics that they wanted to be true about their children in the distant future, they included in their list the following: ability to love and be loved, compassion, connections to others, conscientiousness, consideration of others, empathy, patience, ability to be a role model, respectfulness, and tolerance. These are qualities that will enable their children to become responsible, caring, and contributing members of their communities. And these admirable characteristics are arrived at by empowering children, not pampering them.

> *Gemeinschaftsgefühl:* We act on this sense of connectedness and concern for others by actively taking responsibility for contributing to the well-being of our community.

According to Adler, we pamper a child when we are overprotective and indulge him with too much of our help. In so doing, we prevent him from experiencing ordinary challenges in life by doing things for him that he can learn to do for himself. Such a child is at risk of becoming overly dependent on others and self-absorbed. He may lack confidence in his ability to overcome challenges, not believing that he is capable. And he may develop the belief that he is entitled to "special service."

You can empower your child with special needs and avoid pampering him by identifying the characteristics and life skills he needs to learn, believing that he is capable of making progress toward these, and helping him to develop independence from you as much as possible as he develops these qualities and skills. This means that you have to give him the space he needs to try things, with your decreasing assistance and eventually on his own. It means that he will make mistakes along the way and that you will restrain yourself from rescuing him from making a mistake if his health and safety are not threatened. Keep in mind that the mistakes he makes are opportunities for him to learn.

As we discussed in chapter 10, you can empower your child with special needs and avoid pampering him by providing accommodations for him and by not making allowances just because he is a child with special needs. *Accommodations* is a term used in special education to describe the supports and services that a child needs in order to be successful in the regular curriculum. Accommodations are concrete adjustments that assist the child in learning from instruction and showing that he is learning in spite of his limitations. For example, an accommodation for your child who is nonverbal

> You can empower your child with special needs and avoid pampering him by providing accommodations for him and by not making allowances just because he is a child with special needs.

might be a picture-choice board that he uses to make requests for desired items. You will be empowering him when you make available his choice board and encourage him to use it to make requests. You will be pampering him if you allow him to simply grab the item he wants or whine while you try to guess what he wants. When you empower your child and refrain from pampering him, you will strike that delicate balance in which you recognize that your child needs support in order to learn something and you provide only the amount of help necessary for him to demonstrate success on his own.

From the time Ari was an infant, Mara was committed to empowering him. Earlier in his life when they rode in the car together, Ari depended on Mara to help him deal with the challenges he experienced while riding: his inability to stop unpleasant noises outside the car and his growing overwhelming feelings of upset from having no control over the noises. Recognizing that noises were a source of upset for Ari, Mara decided to give him a favorite toy to hold while riding, both to distract him and to calm him. In doing this, Mara provided Ari with an accommodation that was designed to help him maintain calm even when bothered by noises. Over time, Ari learned from Mara that although he couldn't predict or control unpleasant noises, there were things that helped him feel better.

> When you empower your child and refrain from pampering him, you will strike that delicate balance in which you recognize that your child needs support in order to learn something and you provide only the amount of help necessary for him to demonstrate success on his own.

However, whenever he and Dalia had clashes while riding in the car together, Mara felt conflicted about how to respond and often ended up pampering him at the expense of providing Dalia with fair and equitable support. Mara responded to Ari and Dalia's conflicts by making allowances for Ari that were not helpful to him, to Dalia, or to the situation. For example, when Mara told Dalia to "just give him one of his toys to hold," a toy that had previously been given to Ari as an accommodation now became an allowance. In an unsuccessful attempt to "fix" Ari's upset, which he expressed by yanking at Dalia's hair, Mara pampered him, suggesting that a toy be given to him. In this instance, the suggestion that Ari be given one of his toys to hold was not an accommodation that helped Ari to feel calm or distracted from the noise or his upset. Giving Ari the toy at this stage was providing special service that could encourage future misguided behavior. It did not help Dalia to feel supported and understood by her mother. And it did not increase opportunities for Ari or Dalia to problem-solve solutions to the unpleasant car ride.

The antidote to Mara's pampering of Ari occurred when she pulled into the driveway and reframed her priorities, giving increased attention to improving the relationship between Ari and Dalia. Although she didn't have specific ideas yet for how to do this, her determination to increase harmony in her family was her first step in helping to move Ari closer to the hopes and dreams she had for him. Mara knew that making allowances for Ari by giving him a toy to, in essence, "buy him off" in the moment was not a good long-term strategy. Empowering him to be a problem solver would be much more helpful. Similarly, you will see that the Positive Discipline tools described in this section will help you empower your child with special needs to become a more responsible, caring member of his community.

Put Kids in the Same Boat

All children with special needs are *children first,* regardless of their handicapping conditions. And all children are entitled to experience a sense of belonging and significance and to be treated with dignity and respect. You can empower your children to develop valuable characteristics and life skills if you view them as truly equal to one another, if you value each child no more and no less than any other child. While you hold this perspective about your children, you can also recognize the uniqueness of each child and of his different life experiences.

The perspective of equality among children is especially helpful to uphold when children clash with one another. If children in your family or in your classroom fight with one another, you can treat them equally by putting them in the same boat. Even if one of the children has special needs, avoid the inclination to take sides or to judge who is at fault. Instead, focus on what you hope for: harmony between the children. For your child with special needs, *provide accommodations* if possible. *Listen to all your children,* who will, not surprisingly, have different perspectives. *Give all your children your consideration and empathy. Offer your children opportunities to find resolutions to their conflicts.* And of course, *use communication adaptations* for your child with special needs if necessary.

Mara's focus on Ari's special needs overshadowed her attention to what Dalia needed when the two children were together. She tended to take sides, viewing Ari as the more fragile one in the conflict because of his special needs. As a result, Dalia did not feel listened to or understood; she was not encouraged to come up with a solution that would lead to greater harmony between her and Ari, and she felt hurt and disempowered.

When Mara learns the Positive Discipline tool "Put Kids in the Same Boat," she might do the following:

1. Provide accommodations for Ari.
2. Listen to both Ari and Dalia.
3. Give both Ari and Dalia her consideration and empathy.
4. Offer both of them opportunities to find a resolution to the conflict.
5. Use communication adaptations with Ari during her interactions with him.

Provide accommodations for Ari. First, Mara can provide some helpful accommodations for Ari. She might ask herself these questions: "What adjustments can I make or help Ari make so that car travel is less stressful for him?" "Would he be less upset by noises from the street if he listened to music in the car via headphones or open air?" "If he were taught, in a variety of situations, to cover his ears with his fingers when he hears unpleasant noises, would he transfer this skill to car travel, to help in reducing auditory stimulation and avoid 'flipping his lid'?" "Is it possible for Ari and Dalia to be separated to make a 'neutral space' between them?"

Listen to both Ari and Dalia. Next, Mara can listen to the messages of both children. Ari's message of upset was communicated through his behaviors even without having the words to express it. Dalia's words of distress were loud and clear. By listening to the concerns of both children, with *equal consideration* of both messages, Mara could have responded from an impartial vantage point.

Give both Ari and Dalia her consideration and empathy. Having listened to both messages, Mara could respond to each of her children with thoughtful concern and understanding. In response to Dalia's cry of distress, Mara might say, "Dalia, you're getting hurt, and when Ari does that, you probably feel hurt on the inside too," or "You feel mad that Ari pulled your hair." In response to Ari, Mara might hand him a large picture representing "upset" (or an object that she uses regularly with him to represent the feeling of upset), saying, "You feel upset." Or, if Ari has more understanding of words, Mara might give him the picture or object representing "upset" while saying, "You feel upset when you hear loud noises."

We recognize that, while Mara is driving the car, she will be limited in her ability to communicate effectively with her children. She will not be able to speak to them face-to-face and at their eye level. However, the supportive communication style that Mara develops with both children at home will likely be just as effective in the car, even when she has to speak indirectly and into the backseat while the car is moving.

Offer both of them opportunities to find a resolution to the conflict. While Mara could offer both Ari and Dalia an opportunity to find a resolution to the conflict, their abilities to problem solve, because of their different ages and developmental levels, will obviously be different. Outside the context of car travel, when everyone is calm, Mara might ask Dalia "what" and "how" questions about the challenges of car travel. For example, Mara could ask, "What can you do to take care of yourself when Ari is upset in the car?" or "How can we make our trips in the car more pleasant for you?" Ari, in contrast, because of his significant delays in communication, will need something tangible, with more clear and concrete solutions offered, such as a choice board with options (in two- or three-dimensional symbols) that represent what he could do when upset. Some options to include are "cover my ears," "ask for music," and "ask for a toy." Showing Ari a choice board when he is struggling, and asking him, "What can you do when you're upset?" can be helpful in a variety of contexts, including the car.

Use communication adaptations with Ari during her interactions with him. The communication adaptations for Ari that Mara uses during her interactions involving empathy and problem solving can be tailored to his specific needs and abilities. Ari's teacher, vision specialist, and speech therapist could provide helpful advice to Mara as she designs an individualized communication system for him.

Take Time for Teaching and Focus on Small Steps

One of the most important tools you can use to help your child with special needs develop desired characteristics and life skills is to take time for teaching. As a parent or teacher of a child or children with special needs, you are very familiar with the yearly plans that are developed by you and the other members of your child's team: the Individualized Family Service Plan for children from birth to age five and the Individualized Education Plan for children in kindergarten through age twenty-one. One of the keys to developing a successful educational plan for your child is to identify the short-term objectives that will eventually lead to the attainment of the annual goal. And critical to the accomplishment of the short-term objective are instructional opportunities in which your child learns the small steps that lead to the eventual achievement of the objective.

Initially, as your child is learning the skill that you want him to accomplish, you will likely need to provide help during each of the steps in the skill. As you teach your child the steps of the skill, pay close attention to indications that your child is beginning to independently carry out part or all of the skill. Support your child's independence and efforts to take

> Support your child's independence and efforts to take responsibility by gradually decreasing your assistance as he shows readiness to carry out the skill on his own.

responsibility by gradually decreasing your assistance as he shows readiness to carry out the skill on his own.

When Mara learns the Positive Discipline tools "Take Time for Teaching" and "Focus on Small Steps," she will do the following:

1. Identify skills to teach Ari and Dalia.
2. Teach Ari and Dalia in small steps.
3. Provide more help initially and decrease support as each of her children feels ready to carry out the skill independently.

If her long-term goal for Ari and Dalia is to increase harmony between them while riding in the car, Mara first needs to identify the skills to teach each child that will lead to that goal. Responding to street noises by covering his ears will be an important skill for Ari to learn and will assist in the attainment of the long-term goal. Teaching Dalia to be less reactive to her brother will make her more likely to be helpful to both enjoy the car ride and to be *involved in the useful task* of helping Ari become more settled. She might then show him the pictures or object symbols that represent the behavior he is learning ("cover ears") or the feeling he is experiencing ("upset"). This will have the dual benefit of increasing Dalia's sense of significance as she learns to be both self-sufficient and helpful, and increasing the importance of Dalia's relationship to Ari as she guides him and demonstrates empathy.

Mara can take time to teach Ari, in small steps, the skill of covering his ears to block out the noises he doesn't like. In a variety of situations when he is not riding in the car, she can teach him to cover his ears in response to unpleasant sounds. She can help him by placing her hands gently over his hands and guiding them to cover his ears. While doing this, she can assist fully at first and then gradually reduce support as he starts to carry out the movement on his own. Also, she can use a picture or object that represents the act of covering ears to remind him to do this act on his own, without waiting to hear his mother's words as a reminder.

Mara can also teach Dalia, in small steps, the skill of being helpful to her brother when noises bother him. In a variety of situations while not riding in the car, Dalia can learn to use the picture or object to remind Ari what to do. First, Mara can model the following for Dalia while explaining what she is doing: noticing when Ari starts to show signs of irritation due to an unpleasant noise and showing a picture or object to Ari that represents "cover ears." She can then suggest that they (Mara and Dalia) do it together. Next, Mara can watch Dalia as she does it on her own. Finally, Mara can suggest to Dalia to show the picture or object to Ari even when Mara is not nearby to watch.

With each of her children, Mara should provide more help initially and then gradually decrease support as each is ready to carry out the skill independently. As Ari gets more spontaneous with bringing his fingers to his ears, Mara can use this as her signal to decrease help and provide encouragement. And as Dalia is able to respond with greater independence to Ari's signs of upset, Mara can provide encouragement to her. As Mara's children begin acting responsibly and show care for one another, she can support them through the Positive Discipline tool "Encouragement."

Provide Encouragement

As we have pointed out in previous chapters, you can encourage your child by making positive comments about his responsible behaviors or by expressing gratitude for his actions. Encouragement is the essence of creating "a connection before correction."

Avoid criticizing your child for his misguided actions because criticism will only lead him to feel bad. In order for him to do better he needs to feel better. While it's not easy to encourage your child when he is misbehaving, this is likely the moment when he needs it the most. Encouragement is an important part of parenting and teaching because it helps your child feel a sense of belonging and significance. Encouraging your child will motivate him to do better because, through encouragement, his focus will shift to his responsible actions and will lead him to experience himself as a capable, contributing member of his family or school group. Ultimately, through your encouragement, your child will feel the support he needs to develop valuable characteristics and life skills.

Encouragement would be a useful tool for Mara to use with her children in all kinds of situations, including while driving. If she glances back at Ari and notices him sitting in his car seat playing with a toy, she might say something like "Ari, you really look like you're enjoying that truck you're playing with." If there's street noise and she notices him covering his ears, she might say, "Good for you! You took care of your ears when you heard that loud noise." If she sees that Dalia is interacting with Ari in a caring fashion, she might say, "Dalia, Ari sure seems to like it when you play with him that way." Or if Dalia shows Ari the picture or object to remind him to cover his ears, Mara can thank her for being so helpful.

> Encouragement is an important part of parenting and teaching because it helps your child feel a sense of belonging and significance.

A note of caution is called for here. While this type of noticing can be very affirming to children, parents should avoid commenting so much that they risk making children dependent on them for positive feedback. It is far better when children are focused on their own sense of satisfaction with accomplishing something important.

It could be encouraging to Dalia just to validate her feelings when she doesn't feel like helping. Or Mara could focus on the possible belief behind Dalia's behavior and say, "Dalia, do you know that I really love you?" This could be a real surprise to Dalia if she is expecting a reprimand and could change the dynamics of the interactions between her and Ari.

There are many ways to provide encouragement: making comments, sharing expressions of gratitude, asking questions such as "How do you feel about that?" In using these, Mara will be teaching her children to self-evaluate and to feel worthwhile because of their own efforts and not due to her approval of them.

Show Faith in Your Child Through Your Energetic Support
As you teach your child new skills that will help him develop desired characteristics and life skills, show faith in his ability to be successful. Even if the step in the skill that your child is learning is very tiny (e.g.,

he is learning to hold a cup with a small amount of your hand support instead of your previous full hand-over-hand assistance), let him know through your energetic support that you believe in his capability to become more independent.

What do we mean by energetic support? This is a concept that is used rarely in conventional medicine and mainstream education; it is likely to be given greater credibility in the fields of complementary medicine and holistic education. The concept of energetic support as an effective teaching and parenting tool has an increasing amount of scientific evidence to support its efficacy.[15] William A. Tiller, professor emeritus of materials science and engineering at Stanford University, researcher, and author, uses the term *subtle energies*. According to Tiller, subtle energies of the body are "associated with the directed focus of human intention" and are difficult to measure using today's standard scientific protocols. Yet through his experiments on subtle energies, he has found that "directed human intention can have robust effects in physical reality."[16] In essence, what Tiller and others are saying is that when we project feelings of support and encouragement, our children pick up on this and are helped by it.

Energetic support might also be understood within the paradigm of interpersonal neurobiology, which includes the study of the mirror-neuron system. Daniel Siegel, clinical professor of psychiatry at the UCLA School of Medicine, researcher, and author, has suggested that the mirror-neuron system is the critical part of the nervous system related to empathy. In his eloquent discussion of this phenomenon, Siegel provides this explanation:

> By perceiving the expressions of another individual, the brain is able to create within its own body an internal state that is thought to "resonate" with that of the other person. Resonance involves a change in physiologic, affective, and intentional states within the observer that are determined by the perception of the respective states of activation within the person being observed. One-to-one attuned communication may find its sense of coherence within such resonating internal states.[17]

Within the interpersonal neurobiology framework, energetic support is closely related to empathy. However, while your expressions of empathy are accompanied by words and/or pictures that let your child know that you understand how he feels, your expressions of energetic support will be conveyed through nonverbal communication. This includes, but is not limited to, an eye gaze that communicates understanding, facial expressions that exemplify kindness, and a body orientation that demonstrates openness and love. You convey energetic support through your attitude; children sometimes sense your attitude more acutely than they understand the meaning of your words. Often, the feeling (energy) behind what you do is at least as important as what you do.

> You convey energetic support through your attitude; children sometimes sense your attitude more acutely than they understand the meaning of your words.

Your energetic support will communicate to your child that you have faith in him. Your empathic response will be supportive to your child because it will help him, in Siegel's words, to "feel felt." Children (and adults) who feel felt are far more likely to be willing to solve problems.

Mara can provide regular energetic support to her children. When she helps her two youngest get settled into their car seats, she can direct the focus of her intention by thinking positive thoughts about the connectedness between Ari and Dalia. She can envision how their interactions might look as they relate in a harmonious fashion. And through her nonverbal communication she can be a supportive presence to them both when they are getting along and when they are not. These unspoken thoughts and actions, valuable in and of themselves, will be projected from Mara to her children. Her children will feel them and be helped by them, even though no words have been spoken.

Let Go and Take Care of Yourself

An important step in teaching any skill to your child is the final one in which you step back from teaching and observe while your child accomplishes the skill on his own. As you used small steps in your process of teaching your child a skill, *take small steps in your process of letting go.* In other words, reduce your support gradually until your child feels capable and responsible enough to be successful on his own. If your child makes mistakes that are not going to put him or someone else at risk, have faith that his *mistakes are opportunities for learning.* Letting go allows you to *get a life* so that you can spend less time micromanaging your child's life and more time creating balance in your own life.

While the concepts of letting go and getting a life may be somewhat easier for you if you are a teacher of children with special needs, they might be difficult to even imagine if you are a parent, given the increased demands that having a child with special needs have added in your life. To the parents of children with special needs who are reading this (and to the teachers who spend countless hours beyond their contracted time planning and preparing for their students), we are not saying that you should abandon your child and prioritize your own needs above your child's needs. What we are suggesting is to strive for a balance in your life so that, in addition to attending to the many needs that your child presents to you each day, you make room for your*self.* Spending as little as fifteen minutes a day replenishing your energy through whatever nourishes you (e.g., walking outdoors, reading a book, listening to music) can serve as a reminder that taking care of yourself is as important as taking care of your child. Remember the flight attendant's message: You can't effectively take care of others if you don't put on your own oxygen mask!

> Letting go allows you to *get a life* so that you can spend less time micromanaging your child's life and more time creating balance in your own life.

As you consider ways to take care of yourself in the process of letting go, recall your child's network of support that you diagrammed earlier when identifying your hopes and dreams for your child. Are there people in your child's network who can help you out so that you can take care of your needs on a regular basis? As Mara considers ways to get much-needed breaks from her children, she might think about friends who would be interested in a child-care exchange, even if only once a week. Or she might have a high-school-aged neigh-bor come play with her children for an hour or two each week. Mara will be better able to sustain her-self, as she strives over the years to help her children grow and develop, if she creatively finds ways to let go and take care of herself.

> What we are suggesting is to strive for a balance in your life so that, in addition to attending to the many needs that your child presents to you each day, you make room for yourself.

POSITIVE DISCIPLINE TOOLS RELATED TO YOUR CHILD'S MISTAKEN GOAL

In our opening story, Ari displayed a number of behaviors that were problematic: screaming, throwing his ball, pulling Dalia's hair, and push-ing Dalia combined with further screaming. While the cluster of behav-iors as a whole reflects the fact that Ari was "flipping his lid," let's focus for a moment on the hair pulling, since that is probably the behavior of greatest concern, both because it could lead to physical harm to his sister and because it invited from Dalia a strong reaction that, in turn, invited a strong response from Ari.

As we begin to search for clues about the mistaken goals in the com-plex interaction between Ari and Dalia, we can look first at Mara's feel-ings and her response to Ari as he was pulling Dalia's hair. Mara felt worried about Ari and suggested that Dalia do something for him that he could learn to do for himself ("Just give him one of his toys to hold"). Thus, it is likely that the mistaken goal that Ari was trying to accomplish when pulling Dalia's hair was undue attention, with the mistaken belief "I count only when I'm being noticed or getting special service."

Dalia's response to having her hair pulled (yelling, "Ouch! Stop pulling my hair! Mommy, Ari is hurting me!") was partly innocent behavior pro-voked by the experience of being physically hurt. The fact that she yelled to Mommy about it could be a clue that she was acting from the mistaken goal of revenge—wanting Mommy to hurt Ari for hurting her. Mara's feeling of disappointment with Dalia, communicated by her tone of voice and by momentarily focusing on Ari's needs above Dalia's needs, invited

Dalia to in turn feel emotionally hurt and act on the mistaken belief "I don't think I belong, so I'll hurt others as I feel hurt." Acting out of the mistaken goal of revenge, Dalia screamed at and pushed Ari.

What are the Positive Discipline tools that Mara can use in response to each of her children's mistaken beliefs? For Ari, all the tools described above will be helpful in assisting him in experiencing his sense of belonging and significance as he develops socially useful responses to his car-riding predicament. In recognition of his special needs, these tools from among those described above are of key importance to consider: *provide accommodations* that reduce his sensory overreactivity, *avoid pampering,* and *take time for teaching.*

For Dalia, all the tools described above will be helpful in assisting her in restoring her sense of belonging and significance as she develops socially useful responses to *her* car-riding predicament. Considering her mistaken goal of revenge, the following tools from among those discussed above are significant: *deal with Dalia's hurt feelings* and *demonstrate empathy.* In addition to these tools, it will be helpful to Dalia if Mara *focuses on solutions rather than consequences; creates opportunities for Dalia to develop strong beliefs about herself* ("I am capable," "I can contribute in meaningful ways," "I have personal power and influence in my life") and *holds regular family meetings,* at which time Dalia can put her concerns about her brother on the meeting agenda and elicit help from her family to *generate solutions that are related, respectful, reasonable, and helpful.*

REVIEW OF POSITIVE DISCIPLINE TOOLS PRESENTED IN THIS CHAPTER

1. Identify your hopes and dreams for your child.
2. Build a network of support for you and your child.
3. Empower your child by . . .
   a. Avoiding pampering.
   b. Putting kids in the same boat:
      1) Provide accommodations for your child with special needs.

       2) Listen to all your children.

       3) Give all your children consideration and empathy.

       4) Offer your children opportunities to find resolutions to their conflicts.

       5) Use communication adaptations with your child with special needs if these are needed.

   c. Taking time for teaching.

   d. Focusing on small steps.

   e. Providing encouragement.

   f. Showing faith in your child through your energetic support.

   g. Letting go and taking care of yourself.

4. Recognize that mistakes are opportunities to learn.

5. Redirect by involving in a useful task.

6. Deal with hurt feelings.

7. Demonstrate empathy.

8. Focus on solutions rather than on consequences.

9. Encourage strengths by creating opportunities for your child to develop these beliefs:

   a. I am capable.

   b. I can contribute in meaningful ways.

   c. I have personal power and influence in my life.

10. Hold regular family/class meetings.

11. Generate solutions that are related, respectful, reasonable, and helpful.

13

PUTTING IT ALL TOGETHER: POSITIVE DISCIPLINE THROUGHOUT THE DAY

In the previous chapters, you have seen how Positive Discipline principles and tools might be used with children with special needs. You might be wondering how, in everyday life, you will apply all you have learned. Given the comprehensiveness of the Positive Discipline approach, this could indeed seem like an overwhelming task! (Before you even start, it might be helpful to remember what Rudolf Dreikurs taught over and over: "Have the courage to be imperfect. Work for improvement, not perfection.")

Imagine the process of parenting or teaching your child with special needs using Positive Discipline as a journey. When preparing for a journey, what do you do? Typically, you make special preparations, such as gathering information about the destination and weather conditions, creating an itinerary, and assembling your clothes and other practical items that you will need. Once you have started your trip, you seek out places and events that you enjoy. And should you get lost or otherwise run into difficulties along the way, you are prepared to use the detailed map or first-aid kit that you brought along. You might also have a list of people to visit or individuals to contact should you have specific questions about your travels.

Similarly, when you began your Positive Discipline journey, you prepared yourself by learning about the principles and tools related to this philosophy. You discovered Positive Discipline tools to help you create a home or classroom setting that supports your goals and efforts. You learned Positive Discipline tools related to daily routines and other important events for your child. You learned practical tools of Positive Discipline that will positively influence your interactions with your child throughout the day. You found out that, if you meet difficulties along the way, Positive Discipline's Mistaken Goal Chart will be your "detailed map," providing you with specific tools that will assist you in responding to your child respectfully and teaching her important interpersonal and self-discipline skills. In addition, you learned Positive Discipline tools to strengthen your support network. Through all these efforts, you have available at least ninety Positive Discipline tools that will help you as you proceed on your journey of teaching your child in the most respectful way possible!

> Positive Discipline's Mistaken Goal Chart will be your "detailed map," providing you with specific tools that will assist you in responding to your child respectfully and teaching her important interpersonal and self-discipline skills.

PREPARATION FOR YOUR JOURNEY: POSITIVE DISCIPLINE TOOLS RELATED TO YOUR PERSPECTIVE

In earlier chapters, we described many tools to help you see your child through the unique lens of Positive Discipline. These tools can be available to you at all times, forming a strong foundation for your perspective. This foundation will support and inform you as you interact with and respond to your child at any given moment throughout the day.

Following is a summary of the tools that will enhance your Positive Discipline perspective:

- Understand the brain.
- Identify hopes and dreams for your child.
- Help your child to develop these beliefs:
  - "I am capable."
  - "I can contribute in meaningful ways."
  - "I have personal power and influence in my life."
  - "I have the ability to understand my feelings and can exhibit self-control."
  - "I can respond to the experiences of everyday life with responsibility, adaptability, flexibility, and integrity."
- Understand your child's uniqueness.
  - Know his likes and dislikes.
  - Appreciate his temperament.
  - Recognize his strengths and learning challenges.
- Understand your child's innocent behaviors.
- Avoid mistaken interpretation.
- Provide accommodations.
- Provide communication adaptations.
- Assist others in increasing expectations of your child.
- Educate others about . . .
  - Specialized intervention strategies related to your child's disability.
  - Positive Discipline tools related to your child's misguided behavior.
- Take care of yourself.

KNOWLEDGE OF YOUR SURROUNDINGS: TOOLS TO ENHANCE YOUR POSITIVE DISCIPLINE ENVIRONMENT

Use the following tools to create a home or school environment that supports Positive Discipline:

- **Select an appropriate meeting space.** Identify a family meeting space or a classroom meeting area and chair arrangement that promotes face-to-face communication and collaboration.

- **Create a positive time-out space.** Involve your child or students in creating a positive time-out area including items that will assist with self-calming (e.g., beanbag chair, blanket, squeeze balls) as well as individually selected items that will help your child feel better. Also have available comforting items that can be offered to your child in situations when movement to the positive time-out area is not possible (e.g., if you are traveling with your child in the car or if your child is very upset and any movement to another space, even if it's a positive place for her, exacerbates her upset).

- **Post helpful and inspiring resources.** Hang posters in prominent places in your home or classroom that can serve as resources to you as well as sources of encouragement. Include the following items: the Mistaken Goal Chart, your hopes and dreams list, and inspiring posters that you create that contain Positive Discipline principles. The posters are easy-to-prepare sheets with statements in large print that you place in strategic spots around your home or classroom (e.g., "Take time to teach" posted in your bathroom when you are toilet training your child).

- **Provide communication adaptations.** Make available for your child visual adaptations that increase his independence for taking in information and for communicating his feelings, thoughts, and decisions. Include with these visual adaptations the following: feeling pictures, visual schedules and routine charts, choice boards, the Wheel of Choice, the Anger Wheel of Choice, and a chore/job chart.

CREATE AN ITINERARY: POSITIVE DISCIPLINE TOOLS TO ENHANCE DAILY ACTIVITIES

Daily schedules increase children's sense of predictability about what will be happening in their day. The use of visual schedules and routine charts helps children to develop greater independence because they learn to rely more on the schedule or routine chart for information and less on an adult to tell them what to do and when. Use the following Positive Discipline tools to help your children know what to expect and how to take greater responsibility for their activities at home or school:

- **Help your child learn through routines.** Construct routine charts, with your child's help if possible. The chart will include tasks, usually in sequence, that are part of the routine. Depending on your child's level of understanding, use one or more of the following on the routine charts to represent the steps in the routine: printed words, line drawings, photographs, and concrete items. Visual schedules can be created for the child's entire school day (from arrival to departure) and for the child's home activities (from waking up to going to bed), and/or routine charts can be developed for each of the routine activities that are part of the daily schedule. While not every moment has to be made visual, it's helpful to know that these tools are available and easily made if you need them.

  Routines at home might include mealtime, bedtime, dressing, toileting, family chores, and special time. Routines at school might include arrival, group instruction, individual instruction, lunchtime, personal hygiene, recess, assembly, and departure.

- **Assist your child during family and school outings.** Trips that are outside of the usual daily routines may require individualized preparation for your child with special needs. A printed or pictured list of what to find and put into the cart during the grocery shopping trip can help your child to focus (as well as to make a contribution) while in a store environment that is very stimulating to her senses. Photographs of relatives or friends whose homes your child will be visiting will assist her in knowing the purpose of a car trip. Pictures of what to expect at the doctor's or dentist's office at a regular checkup may reduce fear for your child.

Enjoyable activities can be planned, with your child's input, at family or class meetings by using a choice board with words or photos of possible destinations. Prior to and during a recreational and/or educational outing, you can offer visual information (pictures and/or printed words) to help your child understand the sequence of activities and to make choices or comment on her experiences. A portable whiteboard and marker are handy devices to have available so that communication to and from your child can be visually displayed if necessary.

- **Support your child during the transitions between activities.** For some children with special needs, the "space" between the activities is challenging to self-manage, or leaving an enjoyable activity can be difficult. If you know that your child has a hard time making transitions, be available to provide encouragement during the change in activity and to show empathy if ending an activity brings up unhappy feelings for your child. Remember: Showing empathy means that you appreciate your child's feelings about ending an activity, not that the activity won't still end.

Time is another important ingredient you can add to support your child through the transition between activities. A frequent factor in power struggles and conflict surrounding transitions is parents and teachers simply being too rushed to allow children the time they need to make a change. Children may be willing to do what their parents or teachers ask—but at their own pace, which can be a problem if the adults are demanding that the transitions happen right now, this instant.

Whenever possible, if you are going to make a transition request of your child, do so *before* the transition needs to take place. This will allow time for you and your child to negotiate and reach a compromise together. "We need to leave right now" is a request that leaves no room for negotiation or for choices on the part of the child. But "We need to leave in ten minutes" allows children a degree of choice. They can decide whether to get ready right away and then have a bit of extra time or to continue their previous task for a few minutes before getting ready and leaving.

By being sensitive to your child's need for time before transitioning, and by leaving some room for negotiation and compromise, you can demonstrate and model patience and flexibility. So avoid situations in which there is only one possible course of action your child can take. Obviously, this isn't always possible, but in many cases it is. If you're leaving at four o'clock and you know it might bother your child to inform her at that exact moment, tell her at 3:45 or 3:50 rather than at four o'clock on the dot. This will give you time to be patient and accommodating if necessary and avoid a situation in which your child simply has no choice in the matter.

If your child feels more comfortable predicting what will happen next in his day, your advance warning, combined with an adaptation, will assist your child in making a smoother transition. An adaptation that represents the transition, a picture from the child's schedule board, and/or a timing device will also be quite useful in helping your child to anticipate the transition and in delivering the information in a patient and timely manner. Some children like the idea of having a little timer they can put in their pocket that will "ding" a minute before the time to leave or change activities, especially when it means they can now come and tell *you* that it is time for the change.

PRACTICAL ITEMS FOR YOUR TRIP: POSITIVE DISCIPLINE TOOLS RELATED TO YOUR STYLE OF INTERACTION WITH YOUR CHILD

Among the practical items to take with you on your Positive Discipline journey are tools related to your overall style of interaction with your child. These tools, which you can use every day, will both strengthen the connection you have with your child and assist you in teaching important interpersonal qualities and life skills. While only a few of the tools require that your child have an understanding and use of spoken language comparable to at least a three-year-old, all of the tools can be adapted or enhanced to afford your child greater understanding of and benefit from what you are teaching.

Communication adaptations are visual or tangible props (pictures, photos, drawings, printed words, Braille, and/or objects) that you use to help your child understand the language concepts associated with a tool. For example, a circular board with a few pictures of toy options attached to it with Velcro may be used with some children as a communication adaptation associated with the tool "Limited Choices." **Nonverbal communication enhancements** are the facial expressions, gestures, body language, and/or voice volume and tone that you use to increase your child's understanding of the meaning associated with a tool. For example, positioning yourself so that you communicate with your child at eye level is a nonverbal communication enhancement for the tool "Connection Before Correction." Both communication adaptations and nonverbal communication enhancements help to make the Positive Discipline tools more accessible for your child with special needs and support your child's ability to actively participate in problem solving and learning.

> Both *communication adaptations* and *nonverbal communication enhancements* help to make the Positive Discipline tools more accessible for your child with special needs and support your child's ability to actively participate in problem solving and learning.

The following chart shows examples of communication adaptations for each of the tools associated with your Positive Discipline interaction style.

POSITIVE DISCIPLINE TOOLS	COMMUNICATION ADAPTATIONS
Hugs	Picture and/or printed word "hug"
Encouragement	Pictures and/or printed words that depict your child's helpful actions; pictures and/or printed words of gratitude

POSITIVE DISCIPLINE TOOLS	COMMUNICATION ADAPTATIONS
Time for Teaching	Pictures and/or printed words showing the steps of the task
Problem Solving	Choice board or dry-erase board with pictures and/or words; dry-erase board for problem-solving solutions
Agreements	Dry-erase board for problem-solving solutions; pictures and/or printed words on agreement sheet
Mistakes	Feeling pictures to accompany empathic remarks; dry-erase board with pictures and/or words that offer solutions
Win-Win Solutions	Number board or timer to clarify time expectation; first-then board with pictures and/or words
Kind and Firm at the Same Time	Pictures and/or words on board: "I love you AND__"; first-then board
Mirror	Pictures and/or printed words that show what you observe
Reflective Listening	Pictures and/or printed words that show what you hear
Validate Feelings/Empathize	Feeling pictures and/or words
Compliments	Pictures and/or printed words of gratitude
Sense of Humor	Feeling pictures and/or words
Winning Cooperation	Feeling pictures and/or words; dry-erase board for sharing experiences and brainstorming solutions
Opportunities to Make Contributions	Dry-erase board or job chart with pictures and/or words
Distract and Redirect	Choice board with pictures and/or words
Focus on Strengths	Tracing or photo of child with pictures and/or words related to strengths/talents
Build on Interests	Choice board with pictures and/or words representing interests
Routines	Routine charts and schedule boards with pictures and/or words
Limit Screen Time	Schedule board with pictures and/or words; timer
Special Time	Picture or photo of "special time" with choice board
Jobs	Job chart with pictures and/or words; pictures of job steps
Family/Class Meetings	Family calendar; choice boards; dry-erase board for brainstorming solutions in pictures and/or words

The following chart shows examples of nonverbal communication enhancements for each of the tools associated with your Positive Discipline interaction style.

POSITIVE DISCIPLINE TOOLS	NONVERBAL COMMUNICATION ENHANCEMENTS
Pay Attention	Face child; express interest through facial expression and tone of voice
Encouragement	Face child; position arms open and not crossed; use upbeat tone of voice
Mistakes as Opportunities to Learn	Make "uh-oh" gesture with hands/arms; express caring and concern through facial expression and tone of voice; soften voice volume
Control Own Behavior	Relax body; slow down movements; take deep breaths; use hand gesture to acknowledge lid flipping/calming; soften voice volume and tone
Kind and Firm at the Same Time	Maintain strong, unyielding stance; show compassion through facial expression; use neutral tone of voice and soften voice volume
Reflective Listening	Face child; express caring and concern through facial expression and tone of voice
Closet Listening	Sit/stand in close proximity to child; don't ask questions
"Listen" with More than Just Your Ears	Use all senses to "read" child; face child and observe; in close proximity, feel changes in movement, body heat
Connection Before Correction	Face child; position self at child's eye level; position arms open and not crossed; express caring through facial expression and tone of voice; soften voice volume
Curiosity Questions	Express interest through facial expression and tone of voice
Three Rs of Recovery: Recognize, Reconcile, and Resolve	Face child; position self at child's eye level; position arms open and not crossed; express caring and concern through facial expression and tone of voice; soften voice volume
Make Amends	Change body language, facial expression, volume, and/or tone of voice to reflect love and caring
Don't Pamper Your Child	Face child; wait, watch, and feel for signs of full or partial independence; use upbeat tone of voice

POSITIVE DISCIPLINE TOOLS	NONVERBAL COMMUNICATION ENHANCEMENTS
Enjoy Your Child	Express enjoyment through facial expression, voice tone, and voice volume
Get into Child's World	Face child; position self at child's eye level; position arms open and not crossed; mirror child's feelings through facial expression and voice tone
Build Trust	Face child; position self at child's eye level; position arms open and not crossed; express caring and concern through facial expression and tone of voice
Model the Interactions You Want	Express through body language, facial expression, volume, and/or tone of voice feelings of love and caring
Provide Energetic Support	Express caring and concern through facial expression and tone of voice; soften voice volume; watch and wait for signs of improvement
Hugs	Face child; position arms open and not crossed; express love through facial expression and tone of voice
Sense of Humor	Express delight through facial expression, tone of voice, and laughter

While your use of the above adaptations and enhancements will be helpful for your children with special needs, we have discovered that all children benefit from Positive Discipline tools that are consistent with the nonverbal communication enhancements. In other words, body language, facial expressions, and volume and tone of voice are important. In addition, many children, especially toddlers, preschoolers, and those in the early years of elementary school, benefit from communication adaptations in the form of photos and pictures for the younger children and printed words for the older children.

One important note should be added about nonverbal communication enhancements. Without attention to your subtle and sometimes not-so-subtle nonverbal messages as you interact with your child, there is the risk of inviting mistaken-goal behavior. For example, when asking curiosity questions, it is critical that your tone of voice and facial expression reflect genuine interest in your child's ability to come up with a solution to a problem. Asking a curiosity question in a demanding, interrogating tone of voice (expecting the answer you have in mind) could be confusing or threatening to your child and lead her to shore up her sense of belonging and significance by seeking misguided power. (As a further example, consider the question "What were you thinking?" and imagine how it might be interpreted differently depending on how you asked it.)

IMPORTANT ITEMS THAT WILL BE HELPFUL WHEN DIFFICULTIES ARISE: POSITIVE DISCIPLINE TOOLS RELATED TO TEACHING SELF-DISCIPLINE AND RELATIONSHIP SKILLS

As we indicated in previous chapters, one of the most important decisions you will have to make as a parent or teacher when your child displays a behavior that concerns you is whether the behavior is *innocent* or *misguided*. If your child is acting innocently, in a way that is characteristic of her special condition or her developmental level and/or for a medical related reason, decide what to teach and/or how to provide treatment in order to address the behavior. Further, consider how you can avoid a mistaken interpretation of the behavior. (One way to do this is to make a list for yourself of the behaviors that are characteristic of your child's special need.) Continue using the Positive Discipline tools described above so that your perspective, your child's environment, your child's daily activities, and your interaction style all support your child's efforts to act responsibly and respectfully.

> One of the most important decisions you will have to make as a parent or teacher when your child displays a behavior that concerns you is whether the behavior is *innocent* or *misguided*.

If you determine that your child's behavior is misguided, use the Mistaken Goal Chart to break the code. The following two charts list tools, in addition to the interaction-style tools above, that you can use when responding to specific behaviors related to your child's mistaken goal.

Examples of communication adaptations and nonverbal communication enhancements are listed for the Positive Discipline tools.

POSITIVE DISCIPLINE TOOLS	COMMUNICATION ADAPTATIONS
Teach Children What to Do	Routine charts and schedule boards with pictures and/or words
Small Steps	Routine charts with pictures and/or words
One Word	Picture and/or printed word
Limited Choices	Choice board or dry-erase board with pictures and/or words
Natural and Logical Consequences	First-then boards with pictures and/or printed words
Focus on Solutions	Dry-erase board for problem-solving solutions
Follow Through	Re-present visual information through pictures and/or printed words
Put Kids in the Same Boat	Choice board or dry-erase board with pictures and/or words
Opportunities for Your Child to Be Successful	Pictures and/or words on routine chart, choice board, dry-erase board
Ask for Help	Picture and/or printed words, representing "please help me"
Work on Improvement, Not Perfection	Pictures and/or printed words that show what you observe
Set Limits Respectfully	Timer or number board that clarifies time limit; pictures and/or words on a choice board or dry-erase board
Provide Opportunities for the Constructive Use of Power	Pictures and/or words on a choice board or dry-erase board
Redirect to Positive Power	Pictures and/or words on a choice board or dry-erase board; first-then board
Involve in a Useful Task	Pictures and/or words on routine chart, choice board, dry-erase board
Allow Disappointment/Frustration When Your Child Is Learning New Skills	Feeling pictures and/or printed words
Wheel of Choice	Dry-erase board; pictures and/or words on circular chart
Anger Wheel of Choice	Feeling pictures and/or printed words; dry-erase board; pictures and/or words on circular chart
Positive Time-out	Feeling pictures and/or printed words; picture and/or printed word for positive time-out space

POSITIVE DISCIPLINE TOOLS	NONVERBAL COMMUNICATION ENHANCEMENTS
Teach Children What to Do	Model respectful interactions
Show Faith	Express confidence in your child through facial expression and tone of voice
Don't Give Up on Your Child	Express caring and concern through facial expression and tone of voice
Let Go	Stand back; observe
Act Without Words	Carry out actions with neutral facial expression
Decide What You Will Do	Carry out actions with neutral facial expression
Follow Through	Face child; position self at child's eye level; position arms open and not crossed; observe child with neutral facial expression; maintain voice volume in average range
Message of Love	Face child; position self at child's eye level; position arms open and not crossed; express caring through facial expression and tone of voice; soften voice volume
Ask for Help	Face child; position self at child's eye level; position arms open and not crossed; use neutral tone of voice
Avoid Punishment and Retaliation	Relax body; slow down movements; take deep breaths; soften voice volume and tone
Set Limits Respectfully	Face child; position self at child's eye level; position arms open and not crossed; use neutral tone of voice
Avoid Power Struggles	Remove self if possible, or remain calm and neutral in your body movements, facial expression, and voice tone; keep voice volume in soft to average range
Don't Fight and Don't Give In	Remain calm and neutral in your body movements, facial expression, and voice tone; keep voice volume in soft to average range
Don't Force Your Child	Relax body; slow down movements; take deep breaths; soften voice volume and tone
Withdraw from Conflict	Remove self if possible, or remain calm and neutral in your body movements, facial expression, and voice tone; keep voice volume in soft to average range
Allow Disappointment/Frustration When Learning New Skills	Face child; position self at child's eye level; position arms open and not crossed; express caring and concern through facial expression and tone of voice; soften voice volume

POSITIVE DISCIPLINE TOOLS	NONVERBAL COMMUNICATION ENHANCEMENTS
Positive Time-out	Face child; position self at child's eye level; position arms open and not crossed; express caring through facial expression and tone of voice; soften voice volume
Work on Improvement, Not Perfection	Face child; express interest and caring through facial expression and tone of voice

YOUR RESOURCE NETWORK TO AID IN YOUR TRAVELS: POSITIVE DISCIPLINE TOOLS TO STRENGTHEN YOUR NETWORK OF SUPPORT

Weekly family or class meetings will be one of the most important tools you can use to build a network of support for you and your children. The sense of belonging and significance that is possible during this ongoing and predictably encouraging experience, with an agenda that respectfully and supportively addresses everyone's concerns and strives for win-win solutions, cannot be overstated.

If you are a teacher, you can also use *Eight Building Blocks for Successful Class Meetings.* The eight building blocks include the following goals for your children:

1. Forming a circle
2. Practicing compliments and appreciations
3. Creating and using an agenda
4. Developing communication skills
5. Learning about separate realities
6. Solving problems through role-playing and brainstorming
7. Recognizing the reasons people do what they do
8. Focusing on nonpunitive solutions

The eight building blocks are described in more detail in *Positive Discipline in the Classroom.*[18] As your children begin to learn the steps of successful class meetings, they will develop important interpersonal skills, increased social interest, and improved ability to help find solutions that will benefit the whole group. While some children will be limited in their ability to learn the more advanced building blocks (five through eight), due to their developmental levels and/or special conditions, they too will begin to develop social interest and useful social skills as a function of their regular exposure to the earlier building blocks (one through four).

In chapter 12 we described a method for visually diagramming your child's network of support. If you are in a school setting, be sure to include other school staff and students in your children's diagram, even if your children have limited contact with these individuals. Your children *belong* to the school they are attending, and it is helpful when staff in their school, as well as the other students in the building, welcome their presence. The potential for developing relationships with other children on the playground or in the school cafeteria will be significantly improved if your children's support network extends to other children beyond the classroom. The probability of having your children's needs placed on the school staff's agenda (such as needs related to accessing space in the building or being meaningfully included in the school's special events) will be greatly increased if your children's support network extends to the other staff in the school building.

Finally, support to you personally as you proceed on your Positive Discipline journey is available in a number of ways. Certified Positive Discipline trainers, Positive Discipline trainer candidates, and Positive Discipline parent and classroom educators teach classes and workshops throughout the United States and in parts of Canada, Mexico, Colombia, France, Hungary, Jordan, and Cyprus. The Positive Discipline Association (www .positivediscipline.org) keeps a list of trained individuals who can be contacted to find out about trainings they are offering. In addition, Jane Nelsen, the lead author of this book, has developed a number of useful Web sites where you can access important information about Positive Discipline (www.positivediscipline.com). You'll find encouragement and support on the free online Positive Discipline social networking site (www.positivediscipline.ning.com), where many focused groups have formed, including a "Positive Discipline for Special Needs" group. At this site, parents and teachers raise vital questions and participate in meaningful discussions about how to use Positive Discipline with children and teens.

ENCOURAGEMENT FOR YOU ON YOUR JOURNEY

By now you are probably wondering if it's possible to successfully parent or teach your child with special needs integrating all the tools that you have been exposed to throughout the book. With confidence, we can say yes. We also fully acknowledge that it is, indeed, an ongoing learning process to both understand the principles of Positive Discipline and develop and apply the skills necessary to effectively teach valuable characteristics and life skills to children with special needs using the many tools we have described.

As you look back on what you have read, it can feel daunting, and you may indeed wonder how you will remember, let alone apply, all of these principles and tools. It is neither necessary nor likely that you will commit them all to memory. In pursuing the goals you have for your child, you will inevitably make mistakes, as will your child. By treating each other with dignity and respect, you will each learn from your mistakes. Remember to have the courage to be imperfect. You are a parent or teacher, not a saint. Avoid beating up on yourself when you make mistakes. Learn and start again.

Our hope in writing this book is that we have given you a framework to think about how to raise or teach, and not just manage, your child with special needs. Some of the tools we have described will seem especially relevant to you immediately; these are the ones you will probably try first. Use this book as a reference and a resource that you can return to repeatedly. As is true with a great work of art, different aspects of the Positive Discipline framework will stand out at different times.

In using all the tools we have presented, you will benefit most if you understand the principle behind the tools rather than seeing them as techniques. When you understand the principle, taking it into your heart and using your inner wisdom, you will find many unique ways to apply it. Have faith in yourself and faith in your child. These are the best tools of all.

CONCLUSION

We believe that your children with special needs are capable of positive growth and change. On your Positive Discipline journey, with its long-term perspective and comprehensive set of tools, your children can develop an increased ability to take responsibility for their lives. Along the way they can have deep, satisfying, and cooperative relationships with the important people in their homes, their schools, and their communities.

As you take the principles of Positive Discipline into your heart and use your inner wisdom while you apply with your children all that you have learned, you may wonder how this philosophy fits into the "bigger picture" of the professional community that serves children with special needs and evaluates how well their approaches work. We have emphasized throughout this book that Positive Discipline is a relationship-based approach for assisting children to develop valuable characteristics and life skills by increasing their sense of belonging and significance in their homes and schools. As such, it is in close alignment with two important trends in the fields of education and special education.

The first trend is *family involvement* in the instructional programs of children with special needs. Parents and other family members are encouraged not only to participate in developing their children's early intervention and special education plans but also to partner with school staff to teach their children important social behaviors and life skills both at home and in the community. What is the most effective style of interaction for parents to help their children with special needs develop these useful skills? In a comprehensive review of the literature on the impact of parenting styles on children's development, Dr. Jody McVittie, a lead trainer in the Positive Discipline Association, emphasizes that an *authoritative* style of parenting is most effective both for increasing academic achievement and for decreasing socially unsafe behaviors in children and teens.[19] Positive Discipline, which teaches an authoritative style of parenting, one that is kind and firm and supports the parent-child connection while setting clear limits, is exactly the type of approach that parents of children with special needs can use to help their children develop socially responsible behaviors in the long term.

The second trend in the fields of education and special education is an increased emphasis in school curricula on *social-emotional learning*. The importance of social-emotional learning for improving interpersonal skills and increasing cognitive abilities in children with special needs has been described extensively by Dr. Stanley Greenspan.[20, 21] Positive Discipline, with its strong emphasis on helping children learn social-emotional skills to respond to everyday personal and interpersonal challenges, is, again, exactly the type of approach that can help children with special needs become connected and responsible members of their communities.

Reports of the beneficial use of Positive Discipline (with its emphasis on family involvement and social-emotional learning) with children with special needs are increasing in a large county in the western United States where the seed for this idea was planted in 2001. In the Early Intervention and Early Childhood Special Education program of Clackamas County, Oregon, which serves at least one thousand children with special needs per year, many parents and most of the teaching staff have been taught the Positive Discipline approach. Over the course of the past eight years, parents and teachers have reported successes with their young children with special needs. Even the most significantly impacted children have been helped with Positive Discipline, and their parents and teaching staff have effectively implemented the many tools in this book.

As we shared in the introduction to this book, one mother touched our hearts at the end of a Positive Discipline for Special Needs workshop when she came to us with tears in her eyes and said, "All the early-intervention folks want me to just manage my son. You're telling me I get to raise him." It is our wish that you will enjoy raising and teaching your precious children with special needs.

JANE'S ACKNOWLEDGMENTS

My acknowledgments will be short—Steven and Arlene. I'm not knowledgeable in the area of special education, yet I was very excited when Arlene and Steven shared the success they were having using Positive Discipline concepts and tools with special needs children and their parents and teachers. I immediately suggested they write about it—knowing that what they have learned would be helpful and encouraging to others. This belief was deepened after their first workshop for the Positive Discipline Association annual Think Tank when Aisha Pope came up to them and (with tears in her eyes) shared, "You are teaching me that I get to raise my son instead of just manage him."

Essentially, Steven and Arlene wrote this book. Our agreement was that they would repurpose the concepts and tools from the first Positive Discipline book to illustrate how effective they are with the population of children with special needs. I would then "Jane" it—meaning I would see if I had anything to add. Their writing is so exquisite that I had very little to add.

Then there is Nate Roberson. Every author hopes for an editor like Nate—responsive, helpful, and encouraging. Nate agreed with me about the exquisite writing and had only three suggestions for changes after reading the manuscript.

Positive Discipline is based on the philosophy and work of Alfred Adler and Rudolf Dreikurs, who so firmly taught that all people should be treated with dignity and respect. I am so thankful to Arlene and Steven, who had the vision to see how dignity and respect are translated into the population of children with special needs.

STEVEN'S ACKNOWLEDGMENTS

I have read many times before that any author stands on the shoulders of the ones who came before. I now know this to be true. I would like to acknowledge Jane Nelsen, who made Adler and Dreikurs come alive for me and had the faith to invite me to be part of this project. Jody McVittie taught me that it is always possible to understand Adler more deeply and encouraged me to keep doing so. Arlene Raphael has been a phenomenal writing partner and collaborator; she is a living embodiment of "connection before correction." Nate Roberson, our editor at Three Rivers Press, has shared valuable insights that made me look at our material in a different way. (He really needs to stop saying that he is not a writer!) Janet Dougherty Smith, the recently retired and ever-visionary director of the Clackamas Education Service District's Early Childhood Department, saw the value in bringing Positive Discipline to our program and supported me in making it happen. And finally, there are the children and families with whom I have had the great privilege to work and play. When all is said and done, they have been my real teachers.

ARLENE'S ACKNOWLEDGMENTS

While writing this book, I was often reminded of my fifth-grade teacher, Miss Muransky, who spent countless hours with me after school, during one frigid Chicago winter, editing the mystery novel that I had started. She was the first teacher who acknowledged my creative potential and encouraged me to express it through writing about topics of high interest. For all that she taught me, not only about the mechanics of writing but about the heart and soul of writing, I am truly grateful.

In addition, there are important teachers who provided me with supportive feedback throughout the writing of this book. I wish to thank my brilliantly productive coauthors, Jane Nelsen and Steven Foster, and our highly skilled editor at Three Rivers Press, Nate Roberson. Their insightful suggestions for improving the clarity of the chapters I had written were extremely helpful.

I feel a great deal of gratitude, also, to the Positive Discipline Lead Trainers Dr. Jody McVittie and Jane Weed Pomerantz. Through their inspiring teachings, I have come to more fully understand the wisdom of Adlerian principles and practices.

Added to my circle of great teachers are the children, parents, specialists, educational assistants, and program coordinators whom I have had the privilege to connect with during my many years working in Clackamas Education Service District's Early Childhood Program. Hence, my writing was influenced by vivid memories of the dedicated and encouraging work of Autism Specialist Patty Binder and other members of the Early Childhood Autism Team; the devoted, loving families of the children whom I served; and the young children themselves, "my kids," who taught me so much about how to help them learn.

Finally, I wish to express my deepest gratitude to my husband, Ravid, for teaching me the value of mindfulness, balance, and play amidst a deluge of work; and to my daughter, Leila, for teaching me, through her actions, how to truly give service to one's fellow human beings.

APPENDIX

Praise	Example	Encouragement	Example
Stimulates rivalry and competition	*You are the best in the class at painting sunsets.*	Stimulates cooperation and contribution to group	*You helped Sarah mix the colors for her sunset.*
Focuses on quality of performance	*You hit another home run!*	Focuses on amount of effort and joy	*You are so focused when you're at bat.*
Is evaluative and judgmental; feels good in the moment	*Good boy!*	Has little or no evaluation of person or act; invites self-evaluation	*You kept working on that puzzle until you finished it.*
Fosters selfishness at the expense of others	*You learned to write your name before anyone else.*	Fosters self-interest that does not hurt others	*You sure learned to write your name quickly.*
Emphasizes global evaluation of the person	*You're always so neat and tidy.*	Emphasizes specific contributions	*The room looks very neat since you straightened the bookshelves.*
Sounds good but can make children averse to appropriate risk-taking (*What if I fail?*)	*Another A! I'm so proud of you!*	Inspires children to try (*I wonder if I can.*)	*Your hard work really paid off.*
Fosters fear of failure	*You sang that song perfectly!*	Fosters acceptance of being imperfect	*That is a hard song to learn but you just keep on trying!*
Fosters dependence	*You got it all right!*	Fosters self-sufficiency and independence	*Tell me how you did that.*
Links worth of receiver with behavior/talent	*I'm so proud that you can dance so well.*	Does not let behavior/talent define child	*I really enjoy watching you dance.*
Is often not specific	*You are so nice.*	Is specific	*You shared your crayons.*
Is often not genuine.	*Wonderful! (especially when work is mediocre)*	Is genuine	*Thank you for setting the table. Tell me about your picture.*
Places importance on pleasing others	*I love your dress.*	Focuses on child's interests and feelings	*Your dress has yellow flowers on it. I know how much you love yellow!*

*The authors are indebted to John Taylor for his work on the important differences between praise and encouragement. Parts of the chart presented here are taken directly from this work; see http://www.noogenesis.com/malama/encouragement.html. This contribution, important enough to be quoted by Dreikurs in his own writing,

The examples of encouragement in this chart are just words on a page. As we have suggested elsewhere, tone of voice matters. Children usually know when we are being sincere and when we are not. Accompanying a sincere tone of voice should be a genuine desire to get into a child's world and see it from his or her perspective.

appeared in 1978. Over the years since then, Jane Nelsen and Lynn Lott, as well as many other Positive Discipline practitioners, have enhanced this effort, often anonymously, but usually to great benefit. We include this chart here in tribute both to John Taylor and to those many subsequent contributors.

NOTES

1. Jody McVittie and Al M. Best, "The Impact of Adlerian-Based Parenting Classes on Self-Reported Parental Behavior," *Journal of Individual Psychology* 65 (fall 2009): 264–85.

2. Daniel J. Siegel and Mary Hartzell, *Parenting from the Inside Out* (New York: Jeremy P. Tarcher/Penguin, 2003).

3. Carol Gray, *The New Social Story Book: Illustrated Edition* (Arlington, TX: Future Horizons Inc., 2000).

4. Edward Christophersen and Susan Mortweet VanScoyoc, "What Makes Time-out Work (and Fail)?" *Pediatric Development and Behavior Online,* June 22, 2007.

5. Roslyn Ann Duffy, "Time-out: How It Is Abused," *Child Care Information and Exchange* 18, no. 111 (September 1996): 61–62.

6. Stanley I. Greenspan and Serena Wieder, *The Child with Special Needs: Encouraging Intellectual and Emotional Growth* (Reading, MA: Addison-Wesley, 1998).

7. For more information on sensory processing challenges in children, see Carol Stock Kranowitz, *The Out-of-Sync Child* (New York: Perigee, 2005).

8. For more information on temperaments, see Stella Chess and Alexander Thomas, *Temperament: Theory and Practice* (New York: Brunner/Mazel, 1996). Also see Jane Nelsen, Cheryl Erwin, and Roslyn Ann Duffy, *Positive Discipline for Preschoolers* (New York: Three Rivers Press, 2007).

9. Daniel J. Siegel, *The Developing Mind: Toward a Neurobiology of Interpersonal Experience* (New York: Guilford, 1999).

10. Greenspan and Wieder, *The Child with Special Needs.*

11. Siegel, *The Developing Mind.*

12. McVittie and Best, "The Impact of Adlerian-Based Parenting Classes."

13. Garry L. Landreth, *Play Therapy: The Art of the Relationship* (Muncie, IN: Accelerated Development, 1991).

14. Alfred Adler, *Superiority and Social Interest,* ed. Heinz L. Ansbacher and Rowena R. Ansbacher (New York: W.W. Norton, 1964).

15. David Feinstein and Donna Eden, "Six Pillars of Energy Medicine: Clinical Strengths of a Complementary Paradigm," *Alternative Therapies in Health and Medicine* 14, no. 1 (2008): 44–54.

16. William A. Tiller, "Subtle Energies," *Science and Medicine* 6, no. 3 (May/June 1999): 28–33.

17. Daniel J. Siegel, "An Interpersonal Neurobiology Approach to Psychotherapy: Awareness, Mirror Neurons, and Neural Plasticity in the Development of Well-being," *Psychiatric Annals* 36, no. 4 (April 2006): 248–56.

18. Jane Nelsen, Lynn Lott, and H. Stephen Glenn, *Positive Discipline in the Classroom,* 3rd ed. (New York: Three Rivers Press, 2000).

19. McVittie and Best, "The Impact of Adlerian-Based Parenting Classes."

20. Stanley I. Greenspan and Nancy Lewis, *Building Healthy Minds: The Six Experiences That Create Intelligence and Emotional Growth in Babies and Young Children* (New York: Perseus Books, 1999).

21. Greenspan and Wieder, *The Child with Special Needs.*

BIBLIOGRAPHY

Adler, Alfred. *Superiority and Social Interest.* Edited by Heinz L. Ansbacher and Rowena R. Ansbacher. New York: W.W. Norton & Company, 1964.

Chess, Stella, and Alexander Thomas. *Temperament: Theory and Practice.* New York: Brunner/Mazel, Inc., 1996.

Christophersen, E., and S. M. VanScoyoc. "What Makes Time-out Work (and Fail)?" *Pediatric Development and Behavior Online* (6/22/07). *http://www.dbpeds.org/articles/detail.cfm?TextID=739*

Duffy, Roslyn Ann. "Time-out: How It Is Abused." *Child Care Information and Exchange* (September/October, 1996). *http://www.childcareexchange.com/search/?search=Time-Out%3A+How+It+Is+Abused*

Feinstein, David, and Donna Eden. "Six Pillars of Energy Medicine: Clinical Strengths of a Complementary Paradigm." *Alternative Therapies in Health and Medicine* 14, no.1 (2008): 44–54.

Gray, Carol. *The New Social Story Book: Illustrated Edition.* Arlington, TX: Future Horizons Inc., 2000.

Greenspan, Stanley I., and Serena Wieder. *Engaging Autism.* Cambridge, MA: Da Capo Press, 2006.

Greenspan, Stanley I., and Nancy Lewis. *Building Healthy Minds: The Six Experiences That Create Intelligence and Emotional Growth in Babies and Young Children.* New York: Perseus Books, 1999.

Greenspan, Stanley I., and Serena Wieder. *The Child with Special Needs: Encouraging Intellectual and Emotional Growth.* Reading, MA: Addison-Wesley, 1998.

Greenspan, Stanley I., and Jacqueline Salmon. *The Challenging Child: Understanding, Raising and Enjoying the Five "Difficult" Types of Children.* Cambridge, MA: Da Capo Press, 1996.

Kranowitz, Carol Stock. *The Out-of-Sync Child.* New York: Perigee, 2005.

Landreth, Garry L. *Play Therapy: The Art of the Relationship.* Muncie, IN: Accelerated Development, 1991.

McVittie, Jody, and Al M. Best. "The Impact of Adlerian-based Parenting Classes on Self-Reported Parental Behavior." *The Journal of Individual Psychology* 65 (fall, 2009): 264–85.

Nelsen, Jane. *Positive Discipline*. New York: Ballantine Books, 2006.

Nelsen, Jane. *Positive Time-out: And Over 50 Ways to Avoid Power Struggles in Homes and Classrooms*. New York: Three Rivers Press, 1999.

Nelsen, Jane, Cheryl Erwin, and Roslyn Ann Duffy. *Positive Discipline for Preschoolers*. New York: Three Rivers Press, 2007.

Nelsen, Jane, Lynn Lott, and H. Stephen Glenn. *Positive Discipline in the Classroom*, 3rd ed. New York: Three Rivers Press, 2000.

Siegel, Daniel J. "An Interpersonal Neurobiology Approach to Psychotherapy: Awareness, Mirror Neurons, and Neural Plasticity in the Development of Well-Being." *Psychiatric Annals* 36 (April/May, 2006): 248–56.

Siegel, Daniel J. *The Developing Mind: Toward a Neurobiology of Interpersonal Experience*. New York: Guilford, 1999.

Siegel, Daniel J., and Mary Hartzell. *Parenting from the Inside Out*. New York: Jeremy P. Tarcher/Penguin, 2003.

Tiller, William A. "Subtle Energies." *Science and Medicine* 6 (May/June, 1999): 28–33.

INDEX

A

acceptance, 121

accommodations, 141, 179, 181, 182, 192

accountability, 47

acknowledgment, 90–91, 113, 121

actions without words, 208

activity level, 101

adaptability, 101

Adler, Alfred, 1, 3–4
on *Gemeinschaftsgefühl,* 1, 118, 178
Individual Psychology, 123

Adlerian thinking:
on belonging and significance, 118
on nature and nurture, 84
on pampering, 178–79
on striving for superiority, 122
on time-out, 46

agreements, 203

Alan:
and innocent behaviors, 24–28
limited verbal language of, 11
misguided behavior of, 15–16
in new school, 11–12
Positive Discipline perspective on, 13
striving for belonging and significance, 14–15
taking small steps, 28

allowances, 141

amends, making, 92, 204

amygdala, 34, 35

Andi (Ricky's mother), 81–83

anger, 36, 37, 86

Anger Wheel of Choice, 87, 89, 207

apology, 39, 92, 204

Ari, 171–93
case story of, 171–73
communication adaptations for, 184
empowering, 181
encouragement of, 186–88
energetic support for, 187–89
identifying hopes and dreams for, 176–77
and letting go, 189–91
network of support for, 177–78
and pampering, 178–81
Positive Discipline tools for, 191–92
putting kids in the same boat, 181–83
and resolution, 183–84
and self-fulfilling prophecy, 174–75
small steps, 184–86
visual impairment of, 172

assets, focus on, 62

attention:
nonverbal communication, 204
undue, 17, 18, 146, 148

ABOUT THE AUTHORS

 DR. JANE NELSEN is a California licensed marriage and family therapist and author or co-author of eighteen books, including *Positive Discipline, Raising Self-Reliant Children in a Self-Indulgent World, Serenity, When Your Dog Is Like Family,* and twelve other books in the Positive Discipline series. She earned her Ed.D. from the University of San Francisco, but her formal training has been secondary to her hands-on training as the mother of seven and grandmother of twenty. She now shares this wealth of knowledge and experience as a popular keynote speaker and workshop leader throughout the world.

 STEVEN FOSTER is a licensed clinical social worker who has been working with children and families in the Portland area for over thirty years. During that time he has worked in, directed, and designed a number of treatment programs, always using a relationship-based approach, for young children and families struggling with emotional, social, and behavioral challenges. For the past sixteen years he has worked as an early childhood specialist at the Clackamas Education Service District outside Portland. There he has helped to create the array of services provided to children ages birth to five, and their families. A Positive Discipline parent educator since 2001, Steven is also a certified Positive Discipline trainer, training others to teach parenting classes. He is also a sought-after speaker on working with children and families with mental health concerns.

ARLENE RAPHAEL, M.S. Special Education, is a certified Positive Discipline trainer. For over thirty-five years, Arlene has provided services to children on the autism spectrum and to children with other significant special needs. This has included teaching students in classroom and clinic settings, training their instructors in public and private school settings, and educating their families through parent education classes and family consultations. She has designed and taught Positive Discipline courses for parents and teachers of children with special needs, including children on the autism spectrum. Arlene serves as an adjunct instructor in Special Education at Portland State University, where she supervises student teachers and assists with the development of course curricula for teacher candidates who serve students with significant disabilities.